Real Talk With Real Business Pros

How To Win In A Competitive Marketplace

This work depicts actual events in the life of the authors as truthfully as recollection permits. While all persons and businesses within are real, names and identifying characteristics may have been changed to respect privacy.

Copyright © 2024 by Smart Publishing. All rights reserved.

No part of this publication may be reproduced, stored in a retrieval system, or transmitted in any form or by any means, electronic, mechanical, photocopying, recording, scanning, or otherwise, without the prior written permission of the publisher.

Limit of Liability/Disclaimer of Warranty: This publication is designed to provide accurate and authoritative information in regard to the subject matter covered. It is sold with the understanding that neither the authors nor the publisher is engaged in rendering legal, investment, accounting or other professional advice. While the publisher and authors have used their best efforts in preparing this book, they make no representations or warranties with respect to the accuracy or completeness of the contents of this book and specifically disclaim any implied warranties of merchantability or fitness for a particular purpose. No warranty may be created or extended by sales representatives or written sales materials. The advice and strategies contained herein may not be suitable for your situation. You should consult with a professional when appropriate. Neither the publisher nor the authors shall be liable for any loss of profit or any other commercial damages, including but not limited to special, incidental, consequential, personal, or other damages.

Real Talk With Real Business Pros: How To Win In A Competitive Marketplace

By Jonathan Lautermilch, Renee Lautermilch, Dallas Jones, Marc Mason, Tom Bennett, Stacy Raske, Joseph Compton, David Oltman, Ben Ludwig, Rachele Evers, Brent Knott, Adolfo Ayala, Skylar Sullivan, and Scott Conway

Cover design by Farrukh Khan
Book formatting by Saqib Arshad
Edited by Renee Lautermilch

Printed in the United States of America

SMART PUBLISHING

thesmartshark.com

Real Talk With Real Business *Pros*

How To Win In A Competitive Marketplace

By Jonathan Lautermilch, Renee Lautermilch, Dallas Jones, Marc Mason, Tom Bennett, Stacy Raske, Joseph Compton, David Oltman, Ben Ludwig, Rachele Evers, Brent Knott, Adolfo Ayala, Skylar Sullivan, and Scott Conway

Dedication

To the courageous entrepreneurs forging their paths in the competitive landscape of business:

This book is dedicated to you—the visionaries, the innovators, and the relentless pursuers of success.

TABLE OF CONTENTS

Forward   1

Introduction   3

"You Are So Full Of S#!T!": Embracing Radical Honesty in Sales   7
by Dallas Jones

Elevating Success: Harnessing People and Culture for Competitive Edge   19
by Marc Mason

Beyond Sales: Elevating Your Business Through Building Lasting Client Relationships   27
by Tom Bennett

Foundation for Success   41
by Stacy Raske

Two Years in the Digital Marketing Trenches: How Mastery Paves the Way to Business Success   63
by Joseph Compton

The Power of Connection: Creating a Positive Work Environment   71
by David Oltman

Cultivating a Sales-Driven Culture   79
by Ben Ludwig

Do the Thing that Scares You: The Vital Link Between Personal Fulfillment and Business Success   91
by Rachele Evers

Lessons of Resilience: Navigating Adversity on the Path to Success   105
by Adolfo Ayala

Creativity Sus 'Pen' ded: The Role of Creativity in Business Differentiation and Success   113
by Skylar Sullivan

Unlocking Potential and Empower Others: The Lessons I Learned Alongside Bill   123
by Brent Knott

Unleashing Competitive Advantage: The Power of Growth Marketing for Businesses   135
by Scott Conway

Conclusion   153

About Smart Publishing   155

FORWARD

As a business owner who has traversed the tumultuous terrain of entrepreneurship, I know firsthand the highs and lows that come with the territory. From the exhilarating rush of success to the gut-wrenching sting of failure, every twist and turn in the journey has left an indelible mark on my understanding of what it means to thrive in a competitive marketplace.

In the pages of this book, you'll find a treasure trove of wisdom distilled from the collective experiences of business professionals who have faced adversity head-on and emerged stronger for it. Their stories resonate with me on a deeply personal level, as I too have grappled with the challenges of building and scaling a business in today's fast-paced world.

What sets this book apart is its authenticity—the stories shared within these pages are not merely theoretical musings but real-life accounts of triumph and tribulation. As I read through the narratives penned by my fellow business pros, I couldn't help but be struck by the universality of their experiences—the struggles, the breakthroughs, and the invaluable lessons learned along the way.

Each chapter offers a glimpse into the unique journey of its author, illuminating key principles of success that have been honed through years of trial and error. From cultivating resilience to fostering innovation, the insights shared in this book are as practical as they are profound, offering actionable strategies that you can apply to your own entrepreneurial endeavors.

As you embark on this journey through the pages of this book, I encourage you to approach each story with an open mind and a willingness to learn. Whether you're a seasoned entrepreneur or just starting out on your business journey, there is something here for everyone—a wealth of knowledge, inspiration, and guidance to help you navigate the competitive landscape with confidence and clarity.

May the stories shared in this book serve as beacons of hope and inspiration, guiding you towards success in your own entrepreneurial pursuits. And may you, like myself and the authors who have contributed to this volume, emerge from the challenges stronger, wiser, and more resilient than ever before.

Here's to thriving in the arena of business—and to the journey that lies ahead.

Warm regards,
Jonathan Lautermilch
Chief Executive Officer
Smart Shark

INTRODUCTION

In the ever-evolving landscape of business, success often hinges on the ability to navigate the complexities of a competitive marketplace. Each day presents new challenges and opportunities, testing our resilience, adaptability, and ingenuity. As business professionals, we've encountered our fair share of trials and triumphs, each experience shaping our understanding of what it takes to thrive amidst fierce competition.

In this book, we've assembled a diverse collection of stories and insights from seasoned entrepreneurs, executives, and innovators who have weathered the storms of the business world and emerged victorious. Each chapter is a testament to the power of experience, offering a firsthand account of a pivotal moment in the author's journey—a moment that crystallized a fundamental principle of success.

Those moments aren't always apparent or predictable. While Scott Conway's chapter delves into essential business principles, chronicling his journey through a single enterprise and tackling numerous challenges head-on, leading to a successful exit at just 23, other anecdotes offer unexpectedly personal insights. For instance, Dallas Jones shares a direct lesson on how honesty fosters stronger client relationships.

Rachele Evers' story moved me deeply as she broke free from a cycle of unhealthy relationships to establish herself as a real estate powerhouse. Equally captivating was Skyler Sullivan's adept linkage of creativity to business differentiation.

David Oltman's narrative struck a chord with me, particularly apt for an author guiding others on leading through love, as he underscored the vital importance of fostering a positive and meaningful work environment for team members.

Similarly, Marc Mason reinforces the significance of nurturing a culture of trust and employee development in his account of founding a start-up and turning it into one of Boston's Best Places to Work within a mere four years.

Tom Bennett and Ben Ludwig deliver captivating lessons in effective sales strategies in their respective chapters. Tom shares his transformation from employing hard close sales tactics to embracing a client-focused philosophy that not only saved numerous small and medium-sized businesses from closure but also fostered lasting client relationships. Meanwhile, Ben's narrative recounts a remarkable sales experience grounded in genuine engagement and active listening.

Joseph Compton and Adolfo Ayala's personal stories serve as wellsprings of inspiration, showcasing their resilience in overcoming hardship through relentless learning and adaptability. Their commitment to expertise and excellence paved the way for their future success.

Stacy Raske's narrative demands introspection, urging readers to confront and eradicate self-destructive thought patterns and habits that impede personal and professional growth.

Lastly, Brent Knott's remarkable journey of mentorship is a tale ripe for cinematic adaptation. From learning invaluable lessons from his mentor, Mr. Bill, to discovering his own self-worth, Brent's entrepreneurial journey culminates in a heartwarming "pay it forward" conclusion that is sure to leave every reader with a smile.

From overcoming adversity to seizing opportunities, these stories offer invaluable lessons that transcend industries and sectors. Following each narrative, you'll find actionable tips derived from the author's experience—practical strategies that you can apply to your own endeavors, whether you're an aspiring entrepreneur, a seasoned executive, or a budding innovator.

As you embark on this journey through the trials and triumphs of the business world, remember that success is not merely a destination but a journey—a journey marked by resilience, determination, and a relentless pursuit of excellence. May the insights shared within these pages serve as guiding lights on your path to success in the competitive arena of business.

Renee Lautermilch
Chief Editor
Smart Publishing

CHAPTER 1

"You Are So Full Of S#!T!":

Embracing Radical Honesty in Sales

by Dallas Jones

📝 The Story

As a young entrepreneur, I thought I was invincible.

I was barely 30 years old, was in my third year of running a business all on my own, had already gone through 2 divorces and was raising 3 kids. I figured that I had seen it all, heard it all, and been called every name you can come up with. This meant I could handle any criticism that came my way, especially from people who wanted my help and needed the service or product I offered.

You often encounter this sentiment in those catchy "rah-rah" sales books that hype you up for all the cold calls and door knocking you'll do as a newly-minted salesperson.

"The worst thing they can say is 'NO'."

Let me tell you how wrong that is...

So, I was out there, helping people and hustling, doing whatever I could to get a deal closed. And just like any other day with any other client, I found myself in their living room, chatting about all the latest and greatest technology, and how we can take their old outdated systems and upgrade them to something newer and nicer. They were a referral from a good friend, and we were smiling and laughing together and on the same page about all the possibilities. They had an unlimited budget, spare no expense. They just wanted the solution to be the best so they didn't care about the price.

This is what you would call a "unicorn" customer. And this meeting was going *great*.

On the inside though, I was sweating bullets. This house was by far the biggest and nicest house I had ever been inside, in the richest part of Dallas, Texas. The proposal I was getting ready to write up would be the biggest deal I had ever landed. This one deal was going to be a game-changer for me. The thought of having that kind of money to my name was almost unfathomable at the time.

I kept my cool though, took extensive notes, listened to every concern, and answered every question. We smiled, shook hands, and I left their home that day with everything I needed to put together a solid proposal. They were excited to see what I would come up with, and ready to write the check.

For the rest of that week and into the weekend I took my time searching for all the right equipment, doing my homework, and going over every detail. Here's where we can all relate: the late nights spent researching and ensuring we have everything just right, the phone calls and messages to vendors to confirm compatibility between products and parts, and ensuring that everything will work together seamlessly. Every "i" dotted, and every "t" crossed. I built a rock-solid proposal, then called them up Monday morning to make time to stop by and go over it. It only made sense to me to do this in person. After all, it was the biggest deal of my career, and we're in Texas, where everybody shakes hands.

With everything printed out and all my notes and remarks prepared and rehearsed, I confidently headed over to their house. I was greeted with smiles and usual niceties, and we went inside to go over my recommendations and to "seal the deal" on this project.

We spent another hour or two walking through the place and going over all the ideas and the costs for each part of the project. I am a detail-oriented person by nature, so I was eager to lay out the plan and go over every aspect of the upgrades, and they were eager to listen. The conversation was going well, and I could see the hole burning in their pocketbook as I covered the details. They were ready to go, and so was I.

Then, they asked a question I wasn't fully prepared for. Their question was about repairing one of the pieces of equipment instead of replacing it.

Not a big deal, we got this question all the time. I had done similar work before several times, and had a general idea of what was going on with the equipment. At this point, I had been working in technology for over 20 years and had a good track-record for my accuracy. If you've been around technology as long as I have, you know that most of the time it's just better to replace than repair, and typically the cost to repair is almost as much as the replacement.

During that weekend of preparation I had researched the old equipment so I knew what it cost when it was new, and had prior experience with similar models to give me a good idea of what to expect when it comes to repair costs. In spite of that, I hadn't given much thought to repairing the equipment. During our initial consultation, they acted like they didn't like that piece of equipment even when it was new, so replacing it made all the sense in the world. I figured any talk about repairing it would not go well.

Knowing all of this, I decided to go with my gut and throw a number out there, a number I thought was a "reasonable expectation" to fix this particular piece of equipment.

"It would cost around two thousand dollars to fix that", I said with confidence.

What happened next is ingrained in the back of my mind. It happened a decade ago, and I can still remember it as if it happened yesterday.

"About two grand, is that so...?"

"Yes, that's typically what it costs." The second time, I wasn't quite as confident, but stood by what I said.

The next thing I knew, they were looking me dead in the eye. Then, they said six words that I will never forget:

"You are so full of S#!T."

It stopped me in my tracks. It was like a swift kick straight to the groin. Something us gamers call a "critical hit" – one I had no chance of recovering from. What came next was a brief monologue about how they found the replacement part on Amazon for less than a hundred bucks and that it looked like a simple repair.

After taking this powerful blow to my ego, I did what any normal sales-person would do: I tried to talk my way back into the deal. Of course parts on Amazon aren't "genuine" and come from all kinds of shady sources, and the customer had no idea how to do the repair. Both of these things they were willing to admit. But now, instead of taking my word as gospel, they had doubts about what I was saying. Doubts I couldn't overcome.

At that point, which seemed like an eternity, but likely only lasted for a few seconds I'm sure, I was shown the door and sent on my way.

Just like that, I had blown the biggest deal of my career.

On the ride home, and for many weeks following, all I could do was re-play that conversation in my head. I was looking for something to salvage from this catastrophe. Surely there's some lesson I can learn. Maybe they weren't as ready as they let on and used my slip-up as a cop-out. Maybe I didn't explain myself well enough.

But those six words kept echoing, louder than any other thought I could muster up.

"You are so full of S#!T."

It kept me pinned down. I was in a spiral, swirling down the drain.

Eventually I shook it off and kept on going, thinking I had dealt with it and was ready to move on. Several more jobs and a few big(-ish) deals later, I figured I was back in the groove and doing okay. No big deal, the old mantra of "you lose some, you win some" had somehow started to make sense.

And then, out of nowhere, it hit me again when I least expected it. I found myself in a totally unrelated pit of depression, and that memory came back again, with those six words haunting me.

So I decided to "phone a friend" and reached out to one of my mentors, hoping they could share some insight. Perhaps they would see something I didn't and help me work through this conundrum. What I heard from him was not what I expected, but it was what I needed:

"Maybe they said you're full of it, because you were actually full of it."

At first I got angry when I heard that, but I quickly had a shift in thinking.

He was right.

That customer was right.

I *was* full of S#!T.

Instead of accepting it when it happened, I had covered it up, and now several years later I was forced to face the fact that I had been micro-depositing it into every aspect of my life. Now I was at a breaking point, and something had to give.

At that moment, I decided to come clean.

From that point on, I decided to be totally honest with everyone. No more half-truths, no more white-washing or exaggerating. I was done being wishy-washy with my words.

It was both the hardest and best decision I have ever made.

Let me tell you, as someone who has done a lot of hog-washing over the years, this was the hardest part. I had a reputation for being a smart guy and knowing what to say, even if it wasn't always factual, it at least sounded good and usually made sense.

It was difficult because we live in a world where information and data are right at our fingertips. There's almost this cultural expectation we all have, that we either need to know the right answer or be able to immediately find the right answer. If I don't know the answer right away, then that customer will go find someone who knows it all already, right…?

The pressure to "know it all" is especially present if you are in a competitive market, or a business that most people have a hard time understanding (such as IT or medical or legal). Even if that's not the case, there's something about us as humans where we seem to have an addiction to inflating our ego, and what better way to do that than to appear to be the smartest person in the room?

Being honest with people was the best decision I ever made because I was finally free. I no longer had to remember exactly what lie or half-truth I told to which person, and when. I could sleep well at night, knowing that I might not be telling people what they want to hear, but I was telling them the truth. No more thinking about what to say or how to say it. No more pulling some crap out of my back-pocket to make a point.

I began to learn that "I don't know" was an acceptable answer to give someone. And if I said "I don't know" to someone, it also challenged me to go learn something new and figure it out. I was no longer speaking out of arrogance or foolishness.

At first, it was a shock to people. I even repelled several people, some of which were very close to me. What I realized in those moments though, is that those people were also living in a place of dishonesty, and my truth telling began to expose their phoniness. In the moment, it hurt, just like applying antiseptic to a wound. It doesn't feel pleasant but it's necessary.

The funny thing about the truth is that it is like a powerful magnet. Magnets have 2 sides; one that attracts, and one that repels. The moment I decided to start being honest and stop living a lie, the polarity of my life shifted. What was once clinging onto me was starting to be pushed away, and what was once distant was now coming closer.

That is how it became a blessing. Now I was attracting honest people and building a reputation for honesty. The people who were once repelled by my BS were now more than willing to work with me. Even if there was disagreement, even if I didn't have all the answers, more and better people respected my honesty and sincerity. For the first time in my entire life, my words *meant* something.

This is not some fairy-tale "happily ever after" end to a story, though. It is still hard work to be brutally honest. I can say that I've lost several deals from being upfront with people, and have even had to turn down some lucrative business opportunities and partnerships because they would not have expected me to operate clearly and openly. You might call it "honest to a fault", and I would agree. But I'll tell you what, I can handle those faults, because I sleep so much better at night now.

It turns out that the worst thing someone could say to me, wound up being one of the best things I have been told.

🎯 The Principle

There are several lessons I hope you can glean from my story that have been pivotal in my personal growth and interpersonal relationships.

Honesty can liberate us from the burdens of deceit, allowing us to not only sleep soundly at night, but also eliminating the need to fabricate stories to maintain appearances. Through honesty, authenticity, and integrity, you can form genuine connections with others.

Honestly also dictates the presence of humility. To be truly honest, you have to acknowledge your limitations. It's ok to admit when you don't know something. This simple acknowledgement can transform your interactions from displays of arrogance to opportunities for learning and growth. Humility will also not only enhance your credibility but it can also encourage your personal development by motivating you to seek new knowledge and understanding.

The character you display will also both attract and repel like-minded and unlike-minded people in your life. By embracing honesty, I experienced a shift in the dynamics of my connections with others. While some individuals were initially repelled by my newfound commitment to truthfulness, others were drawn to my sincerity and authenticity. Conducting yourself with honesty has a transformative power in shaping your social interactions and attracting like-minded individuals.

Overall, I hope my story serves as a testament to the transformative impact of honesty, humility, and authenticity in fostering meaningful relationships and personal growth. Living truthfully and embracing vulnerability can be powerful catalysts for positive change and genuine connections with others.

💡 Actionable Tips

Drawing from my personal journey, I've distilled five invaluable lessons that have profoundly shaped my approach to life and relationships. These insights, born from my experiences and reflections, offer practical guidance. Here are the 5 lessons you can apply from my story:

1. **Embrace Radical Honesty:** Strive to integrate honesty into every aspect of your life, from personal interactions to professional endeavors. Authenticity fosters trust and strengthens relationships, laying the foundation for genuine connections and mutual respect.
2. **Embrace the Power of "I Don't Know":** Acknowledge your limitations and be open to learning from others. Embracing humility allows for personal growth and creates opportunities for expanding your knowledge and understanding. Don't be afraid to admit when you don't have all the answers; it's a sign of strength, not weakness.
3. **Embrace Vulnerability:** Dare to be vulnerable, especially with those who are willing to offer candid feedback and constructive criticism. Opening up to others fosters deeper connections and allows for meaningful dialogue. Vulnerability is a catalyst for growth, enabling you to confront challenges with courage and resilience.
4. **Understand the Dynamics of Truth:** Recognize that truth has a magnetic quality, both attracting like-minded individuals and repelling those who are not aligned with your values. Stay true to your principles and integrity, knowing that honesty will attract genuine connections while filtering out those who do not share your commitment to authenticity.

5. **Embrace Second Chances:** Understand that it's never too late to course-correct and choose a path of integrity. Each moment presents an opportunity for growth and transformation. Embrace the power of redemption and commit to doing things right, regardless of past mistakes or missteps. Every positive change starts with a decision to do better, and it's never too late to make that choice.

Connect

Ready to dive deeper into discussions on personal and professional growth? Join my Facebook group today, a place for business owners and those interested in becoming their own boss to learn and grow in every area of their life to get to the next level! Connect with like-minded individuals, share your own experiences, and gain valuable insights to enrich your journey toward success and fulfillment. Click the link to join now! www.facebook.com/groups/mindsetmedic/

ABOUT THE AUTHOR

Dallas is a Jesus follower, husband, dad, nerd, and business owner who has a passion for helping others break out of the mold of mediocrity and live abundantly. He has helped several people on a path to starting their own business and being more effective in their work and home lives. If you want to hear more about his story and see how he can help you level up in your life, visit www.DallasJones.com to connect with him.

CHAPTER 2

Elevating Success:

Harnessing People and Culture for Competitive Edge

by Marc Mason

📝 The Story

Growing up with nothing, I often found myself lost in daydreams, imagining a life where I'd make a mark so significant it seemed like a mere fantasy. Yet, amidst the doubts, the encouragement of my parents and elders echoed: "You can be anything you want to be in life." Though I didn't take their words seriously at first, I understood that if I could envision it, feel it, then I could make it real.

As life unfolded, I discovered my passion for building relationships, eliciting laughter, and witnessing others thrive. High school became my proving ground, where I realized that my calling lay in sales. Starting with humble ventures like selling CDs and phones, I found myself naturally assuming leadership roles as others gravitated towards my vision.

The turning point arrived during my senior year, courtesy of a Co-Op program that melded work with education. It was here that I savored the rewards of hard work and discipline. The rhythm of earning, coupled with the values of respect and work ethic, lit a fire within me—an unyielding determination to shatter the glass ceiling, not just for myself but for everyone around me.

Reflecting on my journey, I recalled my grandfather's words, once ominous, now serving as a catalyst for my ambition. His prophecy of me either ruling the world or ending up in jail fueled my resolve to leave a legacy of success.

Navigating through various roles—from apprentice to project management—I absorbed invaluable lessons in business. Over a decade of diligent work, I meticulously documented every triumph and setback, crafting a blueprint for my future endeavors. Witnessing firsthand the impact of poor leadership, I resolved to foster a positive work environment where appreciation and happiness weren't luxuries but necessities.

The rapid evolution of leadership in the face of technological advancement was starkly evident. Much like Blockbuster's reluctance to adapt to the digital era, companies failing to embrace change risked obsolescence. The lesson was clear: in today's fast-paced world, adaptability is paramount.

In 2019, I embarked on a journey to chase my dreams, founding RCL Mechanical and Eastside Home Solutions. With a vision centered on prioritizing people and fostering a culture of empowerment, my goal was to create a workplace where dreams flourished not just for myself, but for every employee.

Fast forward to the present, and our endeavors have borne fruit. Recognized as one of the top places to work in Boston in 2023, we stand as living proof of the transformative power of passion and discipline. Our company culture, nurtured by a dedicated team, is our greatest asset, propelling us towards unprecedented heights.

For when you have an army of individuals united by trust and shared purpose, success becomes not just a possibility but an inevitability. And as we continue to grow, reinvesting our profits into the company's expansion, we remain steadfast in our commitment to both personal and collective growth.

In the end, it's not just about profit margins or accolades—it's about creating a legacy fueled by passion and sustained by discipline. And as we march forward, we carry with us the belief that with unwavering dedication, anything is possible.

Remember, you can't beat passion and discipline.

🎯 The Principle

Crafting an unparalleled culture isn't merely a business endeavor; it's embarking on a shared life journey with kindred spirits who uphold the same vision and values. It's about forging a culture that commands respect and garners deep investment from all who participate.

In today's dynamic business landscape, the recipe for success isn't shrouded in mystery. The advent of technology, from smartphones to remote work opportunities, has democratized the pursuit of wealth and achievement. Yet, amidst this digital revolution, the key to triumph in a cutthroat industry remains unchanged: dedication, discipline, and unwavering consistency. Within the confines of this section, we'll delve into the indispensable role played by people and culture in sculpting a thriving company primed for industry dominance.

Reflecting on the inception of my home service business in 2019, I quickly recognized the crux of success. Drawing upon invaluable lessons gleaned from past employers and the sage wisdom imparted by a network of mentors, I embarked on a mission to cultivate an organization capable of leaving an indelible mark. In just three short years, our team burgeoned from nonexistence to an impressive roster of 80 employees, firmly establishing our foothold in the bustling New England market. The cornerstone of our achievement lay in a singular principle: prioritizing people.

At the heart of our modus operandi lies a profound sense of humanity. In an era where skilled labor is a rare commodity, particularly within specialized industries, we acknowledged the paramount importance of fostering robust connections with both our team and clientele. By focusing on the simple things in life that people genuinely appreciate, we not only dominated the local market but also devised a scalable framework poised for global replication.

Indeed, each individual is propelled by unique motivations. Nurturing a genuine rapport with employees entails discerning the driving forces that propel them to the workplace each day. Facilitating the realization of their personal and professional aspirations is pivotal to sustaining their passion for the company's mission, thereby propelling collective progress. As organizations expand, there's a tendency to overlook the distinct preferences and capabilities of individual team members. To counteract this, appointing leaders who not only contribute to corporate triumphs but also shepherd individuals towards their own victories is imperative.

In our work experience, we highly value the advice we've received from mentors. Doing well in a tough industry means we need to develop leaders and mentors within our own team. This doesn't just give everyone a clear idea of where we're headed, but it also helps the company do better overall. When people know where they're going and have ways to keep getting better, great things happen because of the strength of teamwork.

A pivotal facet of attracting top-tier talent revolves around fashioning a company that resonates with every individual. Each person seeks a sense of purpose, and by instilling that sense across the organization, you cultivate a company that is positioned for success across multiple industries. Identifying the right individuals for your company becomes seamless when the company's culture and core values align with their personal values. Though each person is driven by a distinct set of aspirations, the underlying impetus remains consistent: a quest for purpose and fulfillment.

A strong company culture doesn't just affect the people who work there; it also impacts the customers. When employees believe in the company and take pride in their work, customers can sense it too. The trust and dedication that employees show often translate into loyalty from customers. So, when employees feel good about their job, customers tend to feel good about the company too.

In a fiercely competitive industry, a business sets itself apart by attracting customers who yearn for a sense of familial belonging. Much akin to talent acquisition, the creation of a company that strikes a chord with a broad audience plays a pivotal role in nurturing a loyal customer base that endures the test of time. After all, beneath the formality of business transactions, we are all human at the end of the day.

Actionable Tips

As we built our organization, we took specific actions to ensure we were dominating our industry and creating a recession-proof business:

1. **Create Core Values:** Establishing core values that align with your vision and mission sets the foundation for your company culture. We begin discussing our core values as early as the employee interview to ensure everyone we hire is the right fit.
2. **Create a 3 and 10-Year Painted Vision:** Clearly articulate a 3 and 10-year vision, showcasing the growth opportunities within

your organization. This helps your team visualize their potential for advancement and inspires them to contribute to the long-term success of the company. This is also something we start to discuss as early as the interview stage.

3. **Showcase Your Team and Culture on Social Media:** Utilize social media platforms to highlight your team members, their accomplishments, and the positive cultural aspects of your organization. This not only boosts employee morale but also attracts the right talent.
4. **Invest in Content Marketing:** Embrace the power of content marketing to establish your brand as a thought leader in your industry.
5. **Create a Brand:** Develop a strong brand identity that reflects your company's values, personality, and unique attributes. Make sure it's a brand that people want to be a part of.
6. **Operate Your Company for Now and Tomorrow:** As you build your organization, it's essential to operate with an idea of what you aspire the company to grow into. Implement systems, processes, and structures that align with your long-term vision, even if you haven't achieved that scale yet.

By implementing these actionable steps, you'll edge closer to your objective of achieving industry dominance and fortifying your organization against economic downturns.

In summary, success in a competitive industry relies on harnessing the power of people and cultivating a robust culture. Prioritizing individuals, nurturing collaboration, and cultivating leadership within your team lay the foundation for a flourishing and adaptable business in any sector. Trust, exemplary customer service, and a servant-leadership mindset serve as indispensable cornerstones for fostering enduring customer loyalty. Additionally, dedicating resources to personal growth, team development, and infrastructure enhancements guarantees the longevity and expansion of your company.

Embracing these principles and executing deliberate action steps will result in a winning formula that distinguishes your company amidst your competition.

Connect

With multiple thriving 8-figure companies under my belt built from scratch, I'm here to empower business owners like you to reach new heights of success. I believe that your journey as a business owner holds immense potential, and together, we can unlock it. Just follow the link to schedule a time to connect: presskit.themarcmason.com.

Also, keep an eye out for my forthcoming full-length book, *The Resilient Entrepreneur*, set for release in late summer of 2024.

ABOUT THE AUTHOR

Marc's entrepreneurial journey has been a thrilling rollercoaster ride, filled with challenges and obstacles. However, with all of his adversity, he emerged stronger and more determined. Marc learned that success goes beyond profitability; it's about creating something of value and purpose. The journey continues, and with each twist and turn, Marc grows, learns, and strives to leave a lasting footprint. This is the essence of his entrepreneurial voyage.

Through his entrepreneurial endeavors, Marc has ignited profound transformations within his community. From creating employment opportunities to supporting local charities and organizations, he holds these accomplishments as badges of honor. Marc is committed to extending this positive influence beyond his community and onto the global stage. Entrepreneurship became his calling, offering a canvas to paint a portrait of meaning and positive change worldwide.

CHAPTER 3
Beyond Sales:
Elevating Your Business Through Building Lasting Client Relationships

by Tom Bennett

The Story

Among the multitude of sales professionals, the consistent skill that elevates the good from the great is the ability to sell with a servant heart. It's not merely about pitching a product or service believed in, but also about serving and supporting clients at the highest level. Those who excel in this capacity are the consultants and advisors who wake up each morning with an infectious excitement, propelled by the knowledge that they can positively impact the world while finding genuine joy and purpose in their work. There's a stark contrast between genuinely serving clients with a steadfast commitment to their success and relying solely on aggressive closing techniques to secure deals. Personally, I've come to believe that confidence in the positive impact of one's products and services on customers' businesses is paramount; without it, one cannot reach their full potential, a lesson I learned the hard way.

For nearly a decade, I've collaborated with numerous business owners across industries and of varying sizes, navigating through experiences and stories that span the spectrum. From large corporate entities to startups, and everything in between, my journey has been diverse, offering a wealth of insights to share.

Along my sales journey, I've encountered numerous challenges. I've had the police called on me, faced threats, endured slammed doors, weathered a barrage of insults, and even had dogs unleashed upon me in attempts to drive me away while soliciting.

My journey in sales began at the age of 22. Prior to that, I had been immersed in the food service industry, steadily climbing the ranks to a supervisory position. However, a desire to venture into the business world, particularly sales, had been brewing within me.

At that juncture, my perception was that the only route into sales was through a college education, a notion I'd been consistently fed. As luck would have it, a close friend approached me with an opportunity to interview at SolarCity, a prominent solar energy company. Securing the position, I delved into the world of door-to-door solar sales, marking the genesis of my sales education.

The sales domain has often been tarnished by a negative reputation, largely due to the pervasive use of aggressive sales and closing techniques. Phrases like "Close early and close often" or the mantra "ABC" (Always Be Closing), along with portrayals in films like *The Wolf of Wall Street* and *Boiler Room*, have contributed to this stigma. Moreover, the prevailing wisdom was to knock on a minimum of 100 doors daily, constituting the extent of my initial sales training.

Determined to refine my skills, I embarked on a journey of self-improvement, diving into literature by luminaries such as Brian Tracy, and consuming audio recordings by industry stalwarts like Tom Hopkins and Zig Ziglar. Eventually, I gained access to sales training programs led by Grant Cardone and Jordan Belfort, whose "Straight Line Persuasion" philosophy underscored a resolute refusal to accept rejection.

At this point, I adopted a pushy and assertive sales approach, aligning with the methods I had been taught. My sales journey persisted as I transitioned to selling Power Purchase Agreements (PPA), a model wherein the solar company assumed responsibility for installing and maintaining panels on the customer's roof. Under this arrangement, homeowners committed solely to purchasing the solar electricity generated at a fixed rate over a predetermined period, typically spanning 10 to 25 years. As this constituted a lease program, I was precluded from extolling the benefits of solar ownership; instead, my focus shifted to illustrating how homeowners in affluent Massachusetts towns could economize on their monthly utility bills.

Invariably, the predominant response I encountered was resistance grounded in concerns over aesthetics or perceived savings insufficiency. Frequently, it was a combination of both factors. While I occasionally managed to surmount these objections, the process failed to evoke joy or excitement.

Operating on a commission basis and lacking prior sales experience, I experienced fluctuations in income, with some months proving lucrative while others posed challenges in meeting financial obligations. Subsequently, I accepted a position at one of the largest uniform service companies, perpetuating the theme of refusing to accept rejection, albeit on a grander scale. Yet again, I found myself selling services that failed to instill confidence or passion.

Eventually, I transitioned to HR, payroll, and timekeeping sales, marking a pivotal moment where I began to believe in the products I represented. While recognizing that belief alone is insufficient for success, it served as a foundational element. Indeed, one cannot effectively serve clients or achieve success without genuine enthusiasm and conviction in the offerings being sold.

In 2019 and 2020, amidst the global outbreak of Covid-19, the ensuing pandemic wreaked havoc on businesses of all sizes, from small enterprises to larger corporations. During this period, I was engaged in selling HR, payroll, and time tracking systems to schools across the nation, covering a vast expanse stretching from Maine to Mississippi, encompassing a multitude of educational institutions.

As I navigated through my daily routines, the distressing sight of businesses shuttering their doors left and right cast a depressing tone. The impact of the pandemic hit home when, during the final stages of negotiation for what promised to be my most significant deal to date, a superintendent informed me that the institution's budget had been slashed by $350,000.

In that moment, the gravity of the pandemic's reach dawned on me, prompting me to quickly adapt. Recognizing the far-reaching implications beyond the educational sector, I underwent a profound shift in my motivation. I resolved to pivot my focus exclusively to aiding small and medium-sized enterprises, not only in weathering the storm of the pandemic but also in thriving and realizing their organizational and personal objectives. Demonstrating to clients how my services could assist them in achieving both their business and personal aspirations became paramount.

Amidst the challenging landscape, it became evident that businesses were in dire need of two critical elements: financial resources and additional support.

The closure of numerous businesses due to financial constraints and a lack of adequate resources is a stark reminder of the potential impact I could have made. Providing assistance in the form of business tax credits, working capital, lines of credit, and other financial resources could have potentially altered the course for many struggling enterprises.

In addressing the issue of resource scarcity, it became evident that there were numerous programs available to support businesses, yet many business leaders remained unaware of their existence. Programs such as the Paycheck Protection Program (PPP), Economic Injury Disaster Loan (EIDL), The Restaurant Revitalization Fund, Employee Retention Tax Credit (ERC / ERTC), Shuttered Venue Operators Grant, and SBA Debt Relief were among the initiatives aimed at aiding businesses. However, the absence of proactive outreach from organizations like the IRS left many entrepreneurs uninformed or misinformed about their eligibility and conversely, they missed out on valuable opportunities.

A prevailing misconception encountered was the belief that businesses could only qualify for either PPP or ERC, unaware of the updated guidelines allowing eligibility for both, provided there was no double-dipping on wages. As the challenges mounted, it became increasingly apparent that clients needed support more than ever, particularly in the wake of the Covid-19 pandemic, which adversely impacted the vast majority of small and medium-sized enterprises. This fueled my determination to intervene and assist clients in accessing PPP, EIDL, ERC funding, and any other resources or assistance they needed.

After navigating through six corporate sales roles, I came to the realization that the corporate environment was not conducive to my approach. Focused solely on closing deals swiftly, the prevailing ethos clashed with my ethos of prioritizing client relationships and providing tailored solutions. Embracing a sales approach characterized by a servant heart became my defining philosophy, setting me apart in the field and ultimately yielding greater satisfaction in my work.

Don't get me wrong, selling undoubtedly plays a pivotal role in driving bottom-line results, but there's a more effective approach to sales that often goes overlooked. In the corporate realm, roles are typically divided between account executives, responsible for generating new business, and account managers, tasked with nurturing existing client relationships and driving upsells. Recognizing the value of both functions, I sought to integrate elements of both into my approach.

Amidst the challenges of the pandemic, I came to realize the immense need for support among businesses that often went unmet. This realization prompted me to shift my focus towards building partnerships with consultants offering a diverse range of products and services. Rather than fixating solely on promoting our offerings, my interactions with prospects and clients centered around understanding their challenges and identifying how their businesses could benefit.

Through networking groups, I discovered organizations dedicated to supporting small and medium-sized businesses during these challenging times. Their unwavering commitment to finding solutions for businesses impacted by Covid-19 inspired me. Witnessing the tangible impact they were making on countless lives and businesses, I recognized that I had yet to realize my full potential. It became clear to me that my calling was to contribute to keeping businesses afloat and propelling them towards success.

With this newfound purpose, I transitioned from a corporate sales role to a position with a small firm focused on simplifying the lives of business owners. This shift marked a significant turning point in my career, as I evolved from being a mere salesman to a trusted consultant and advisor.

🎯 The Principle

Believing in what you sell and understanding your "why" can give you a significant edge over other sales representatives. The effectiveness of your sales process and outcomes hinges on the quality of the questions you ask prospective clients and your genuine concern for their business. Many salespeople fall short because they prioritize rushing through the process to close deals quickly, neglecting the importance of thorough questioning.

Shifting your focus to serving your clients and finding the best solutions for them transforms closing a deal into a simple agreement to proceed, leading to problem-solving. By asking insightful questions and prioritizing client education over closing tactics, you position yourself to outperform the competition.

Service is arguably the most underrated yet crucial skill for a salesperson. Adopting a mindset of selling with a servant heart can revolutionize your approach and yield substantial improvements in business outcomes.

A helpful perspective is to tune into "WII-FM," which stands for "What's in it for me?" This involves putting yourself in the client's shoes and focusing on meeting their needs and desires. When you genuinely connect with your clients, prioritize their interests, and offer value, success naturally follows.

When you adopt the mindset that you work for your clients and strive to enhance their business, your results will reflect that commitment. Putting your prospect's interests first ensures their success, which ultimately contributes to your own. Satisfied clients are more likely to provide referrals, further fueling your success.

The number and quality of clients you serve directly correlate with your success. By delivering value and understanding that clients seek outcomes, not just products or services, you position yourself and your client to win.

However, customer focus alone isn't sufficient. It's crucial to have an in-depth understanding of your products and services and how they can address your clients' needs. Providing targeted solutions and demonstrating empathy are essential components of success.

Empathy, the ability to understand and share others' feelings, is a powerful tool. When combined with confidence and a servant seller approach, it becomes a potent force for helping clients overcome challenges. Being outcome-focused allows you to prioritize the best possible results for your clients, resulting in a fulfilling experience for both parties.

One of my favorite quotes comes from the great Zig Ziglar: "You can have everything in life you want if you will just help enough people get what they want." I wholeheartedly embrace this philosophy because focusing on the client's success ultimately benefits everyone involved.

Instead of adhering strictly to the "Always Be Closing" mantra, I prioritize "Always Be Servicing." By obsessing over the best outcomes for my clients, displaying humility, and setting aside ego, both the client and I emerge victorious.

Shifting to a mindset of selling with a servant heart has ignited my passion for helping clients lead better lives and achieve their business and personal goals. I recognize that many salespeople may feel constrained by quotas and metrics, but nurturing relationships, asking insightful questions, and truly understanding clients and their businesses are essential for long-term success.

Relying solely on short-term sales results is insufficient for achieving lasting progress. Investing time in asking probing questions during discovery calls, understanding clients' concerns, frustrations, and aspirations, and determining how your products or services align with their needs is crucial for building meaningful relationships and driving sustainable growth.

I make a point to be transparent with prospects from our first call, informing them if I don't believe our offering aligns well with their needs and then directing them to someone who can provide exactly what they require for their business. Every product or service should address your clients' wants and needs, offering a solution that positively impacts them.

Educating prospects rather than solely focusing on selling is crucial. As an advisor, I aim to help them understand what's best for their situation and how we can achieve their desired outcomes. My ultimate goal is to leave clients in a better position than when our initial conversation began.

Asking insightful questions and delving deep into your clients' needs is essential. Thoughtfully prepared questions enable you to gain a comprehensive understanding of your clients and their business, allowing you to tailor the best solution for them. There's a stark contrast between actively listening to your prospect's responses and merely moving on to the next question, a trait common among many sales representatives.

Emphasizing question-based selling and attentive listening leads to positive results. Genuine care and active listening can preempt nearly every objection, as clients will freely express their needs and preferences, guiding the sales process. The quality of your questions directly impacts the quality of your prospect's responses, providing valuable insights into their pain points and challenges and guiding you toward the best outcomes. By asking the right questions, staying silent, and truly listening, you gain comprehensive knowledge about your client and their needs.

Being fully present for your prospects is essential. This shift was monumental for me, contrary to the training I received and the typical sales approaches I had adopted. Earning a client's trust hinges on three factors: they must know, like, and trust you, with trust being the linchpin. Selling with a servant heart, prioritizing their needs over yours, naturally fosters trust. Building trust doesn't require a long time; it can be cultivated through preparation, empathy, and a genuine interest in serving your client. Once trust is established, clients are likely to remain loyal unless one of these factors diminishes.

Many sales representatives remain at Level 1, sticking to surface-level questions like "how's the market" or "how's your business," without delving deeper into meaningful business discussions. While basic questions are common, it's the strategic, deeper inquiries that uncover a prospect's pain points and challenges.

Focusing on your customers' needs not only increases customer loyalty, satisfaction, retention, and referrals but also earns repeat business. Succeeding is simple when you genuinely care about your customers' needs and strive for their best outcome. Doing right by your client often leads to them reciprocating, fostering lasting, profitable relationships and generating referrals and repeat business. Shifting the mindset to prioritize the customer's outcome is crucial for salespeople aiming for long-term success.

Another underrated skill among sales representatives is preparation. The more prepared you are to assist your prospect or client, the better the outcome. Unfortunately, many salespeople claim they lack time for training, preparation, and improvement, akin to an athlete saying they don't have time for the gym. In today's world, most prospective clients have already done their research and know what they want. Your job is to listen and help them achieve their goals. When a client is more prepared than you, you've already put yourself at a disadvantage. It's crucial to understand the fine line between selling and serving. Many salespeople overlook research throughout the sales cycle, especially before initial outreach, which can make a significant difference. Why would a customer want to do business with you if you know nothing about them or their business? Aim to exceed expectations and always do more than necessary for your clients. It's better to under-promise and over-deliver or set the right expectations from the start. Zig Ziglar's quote, "When you do more than you're paid to do, you will eventually be paid more for what you do," rings true.

When you sell with a servant heart, you naturally earn repeat and referral business, testimonials, and various upsells and renewals. This ensures you hit your targets almost automatically. Given that client acquisition is the most expensive aspect for small business owners, retaining clients you've earned is paramount. Regular check-ins, updates, seeking feedback, handling complaints, and seeking referrals or testimonials are essential. While average salespeople spend minimal time asking questions, exceptional advisors engage in intellectual business conversations, understanding the prospect's business, challenges, and needs before offering tailored solutions. Sales essentially boils down to problem-solving; your job is to meet or exceed your clients' needs, positioning yourself not just as a vendor, but as a trusted helper and problem-solver.

By prioritizing service over sales, we foster healthier business environments and enrich customer relationships. Selling with a servant heart means focusing on ensuring your prospects win in every sale, developing mutually beneficial relationships, and putting customers' interests above your own. As Theodore Roosevelt aptly said, "Nobody cares how much you know until they know how much you care." Embrace a customer-first mindset and sell with a servant heart, remembering that the more you give, the more you receive.

The bottom line is that selling with a servant heart positions you to better assist your clients and reach your true potential by prioritizing their needs over your own. When you shift your focus to ensuring your clients win, you ultimately work for their benefit, yielding the best results. I recommend embracing a customer-first mindset and selling with a servant heart—it's as simple as giving more to earn more.

💡 Actionable Tips

The principles outlined in the preceding section are actionable, yet if I were to distill them to their essence, here's the fundamental advice I'd offer to anyone engaging in client sales.

1. Lead with a servant focus. Your goal is to help your client win, and as a result, you too will win.
2. Listen attentively to your client without formulating your response in advance. Focus on understanding their needs and future desired state.
3. Pay attention to what is not being said and delve deeper to uncover hidden concerns or preferences.
4. Maintain laser focus on your prospect's responses to your questions; their feedback will provide valuable insights into their frustrations, desires, and goals.
5. Ask probing questions to gain a comprehensive understanding of your customer's needs, pains, and aspirations. Aim to become a sales "doctor" by meticulously exploring their requirements.
6. Each question you ask should bring you closer to understanding the client's true needs and objectives.
7. Focus on delivering what the client wants and strive to fulfill their expectations, guiding them towards their desired future state.
8. Utilize a Customer Relationship Management (CRM) system to track prospect and client information, including important dates

like birthdays and anniversaries. Additionally, record their preferences and interests to personalize your interactions and build stronger relationships over time.

Connect

If you're eager to accelerate your journey to selling with a servant heart, join our team and learn the recipe directly from me, absolutely FREE. Don't hesitate to reach out and partner with me to discover how to sell with genuine care.

Additionally, visit growwithfunding-taxcredits.com to determine if a quick call could propel your business to new heights! Also, be sure to tune in to the *Small Business, Big Moves* Podcast, available on all platforms.

ABOUT THE AUTHOR

I'm Tom Bennett, a business consultant at TMB Consulting Group in collaboration with Shield Advisory Group. Our expertise lies in driving business growth, spanning from securing funding to maximizing tax credits and everything in between. With nearly a decade of experience, I've had the privilege of partnering with countless small to medium-sized business owners like yourself. Let's work together to take your business to new heights.

CHAPTER 4

Foundation for Success

by Stacy Raske

📝 The Story

James Clear once said, "You do not rise to the level of your goals. You fall to the level of your systems."

Here's a little secret no one tells you when starting a business: entrepreneurship will persistently trigger all of your deepest wounds, fears, and bullshit beliefs. Living a life filled with constant uncertainty, outside of your comfort zone, means your primitive survival brain will keep you trapped in stressful cycles of fight, flight, freeze, or fawn. This means that if you're not learning how to manage yourself, your stress, and your emotions, you'll never reach your big goals. Like all entrepreneurs, I had big goals and pieces of a plan. What I wasn't prepared for was what it would actually take to reach my goals and achieve consistent success over time.

I started my business from a simple idea of what I thought it could be, or perhaps thought it *should* be. Despite all the work I'd already done on myself during my trauma and addiction recovery journey, I wasn't prepared to feel like I was starting all over again. Navigating the process of building my business constantly triggered my tendencies towards self-sabotage and ineffective coping mechanisms. Almost immediately, I found myself battling my inner critic, my tendencies towards perfection and procrastination, and other control issues. This caused me to self-soothe with things that gave me a dopamine hit, like checking social media or other distractions. The biggest problem was jumping into action without giving myself a clear direction or crafting a plan, so I would just hyper-focus on something that interested me, like building my website or designing a post or funnel, rather than engaging in revenue-generating activities. In truth, my lack of effective self-management skills translated into neglecting to establish a strong foundation for both myself and my business, let alone effectively managing it.

My first year in business, I had no idea what I was doing. Despite acquiring a few clients and increasing the investment for my programs as my confidence grew, I knew I was capable of more. At the time, I wasn't aware of how bad my control issues were getting. Perfectionism, procrastination, judgment, and high expectations were beginning to exert their toll, with impatience notably taking its toll.

I began seeking a solution to address my revenue challenges, initially attributing them to potential marketing and conversion issues, despite not actively engaging in lead generation or communication efforts. This was a significant step for me, given my reluctance to seek assistance—an aspect of my struggle with control. After weeks of research, I finally clicked on an advertisement, attended a webinar, and scheduled a sales call. Despite recognizing the sales pitch, I felt desperate and decided to make the deposit. At that moment, I convinced myself that this program held the solution to my business woes, offering the promise of consistent revenue generation at last.

A few weeks later, I maxed out two credit cards to pay the $10,000 fee. What I didn't realize, along with not knowing what I didn't know, was that I was putting the responsibility for my success on the program rather than on myself. Plus, I was seeking an external solution to address my problems and rescue my business, as well as myself, from failure. This was compounded by my husband's escalating concerns regarding my costly and time-consuming hobby, which I referred to as my business. Like all big goals and ideas, I was all in at the beginning. That is, until it got hard. Very quickly, I realized the program I had enrolled in was moving too quickly for my habits of perfectionism, procrastination, and avoidance. Hustling to move forward only worked for a short time, until my self-sabotage became so strong that I didn't complete the eight-week program at all. I was completing the tasks in the program for the sake of completing tasks, but it was nothing more than busyness and box-checking. I was missing the clarity and confidence I needed to build true success.

You see, regardless of the size of my goals and dreams, my daily habits didn't align with success. I neglected personal development, including mindset, self-leadership, and success habits, allowing my unhealthy coping mechanisms to persist unchecked, ultimately undermining myself and my aspirations. I spent so much time working *in* and *on* my business that there was no time or energy for anything else. All that hustle led to burnout and overwhelm with no ROI. Plus, it negatively impacted my health and marriage. I need to work to improve

- my beliefs around money and value,
- my daily habits and routines to build confidence in my self-leadership,
- my ability to create boundaries around time and energy so I didn't overwork, and
- how I managed my stress levels so I didn't default to control or unhealthy self-soothing like distraction, avoidance, or procrastination.

Instead of channeling my energy into meaningful goals that would support my success, I mistakenly focused on proving my worth through unproductive daily habits and routines. It wasn't until later that I realized success is determined by my floor, not my ceiling. I'll delve into this concept further in this chapter.

🎯 The Principle

Symptoms

Your current foundation is constructed from the coping skills and habits instilled in you during your upbringing by your family of origin. These elements dictate your standards for success and sabotage (your ceiling and floor), as well as your ability to alter them. This blend of learned behaviors and coping mechanisms, perhaps honed to survive dysfunction, has brought you to this point—a noteworthy achievement rather than a cause for criticism. However, these skills and behaviors no longer serve your aspirations. While some individuals possess a robust foundation capable of weathering any challenge, many do not. Their foundation resembles a game of Jenga, where the absence of key pieces becomes increasingly apparent over time, signaling that their existing resources won't facilitate further growth. This instability breeds a subconscious desire for control over uncontrollable aspects of life, perpetuating cycles of self-doubt, sabotage, inconsistency, and instability. Consequently, you're left feeling burnt out, drained, and overwhelmed, yet feeling like you got nothing done. It's akin to constantly extinguishing fires rather than preventing them from igniting in the first place.

Building a lasting empire on an unstable foundation is akin to constructing a castle on sand—it's only a matter of time before it crumbles. Despite outward appearances, you can sense the underlying instability, with fear, doubt, and insecurity seeping through the cracks. No amount of hustle or attempts to control the situation can halt the inevitable. I refer to this phenomenon as "Hiding in the Hustle." It involves masking problems with sabotage and distraction while projecting a façade of confidence, whether through a forced smile or curated social media posts. In essence, it's pretending everything is fine when it's anything but. The "fake it till you make it" mantra won't suffice here. Instead, it exacerbates control issues, perpetuates cycles of self-sabotage, and emboldens the inner critic.

Let's explore control issues a bit deeper, as they can be more insidious and harmful than one might realize. You're likely acquainted with concepts like perfectionism and procrastination, both of which originate from a desire to influence the outcome of your endeavors to control others' perceptions and emotions toward you. Perfectionism fixates on achieving flawless performance or outcomes, while procrastination often arises from a belief that conditions must be perfect before starting or that a project must be perfect before it's considered complete. In essence, procrastination is just another form of perfectionism. Additionally, perfectionists tend to avoid situations where success isn't guaranteed, which can be particularly problematic in business, where uncertainty is unavoidable.

There are several other control issues that often go unnoticed but can be just as detrimental to your success. Firstly, there are expectations, where you attempt to control things in your mind, such as people and outcomes. The issue of judgment stems from our tendency to constantly assess ourselves and others, noticing every flaw, in an attempt to protect ourselves or others from criticism. Essentially, you're preemptively judging others before they have the chance to judge you, thereby maintaining a sense of separation and safety in the relationship.

Hustle is essentially a control issue, driven by the belief that increased action will yield desired outcomes, even if those outcomes are beyond your control. The narrative goes, "If I just work harder, I'll achieve my goals." This mindset hinges on the idea that one's value and sufficiency are solely linked to productivity and activity. However, it often results in a cycle of busyness rather than genuine productivity, neglecting the need for rest and balance in life. This imbalance can lead to burnout and exhaustion. The pervasive hustle culture exacerbates these issues, perpetuating cycles of overwork, followed by burnout, which ultimately undermines long-term consistency and success.

One of the most surprising control issues that often catches people off guard is the concept of giving. You might wonder, how could giving possibly be a control issue? Well, if you excel at giving but struggle with receiving, you've essentially turned giving into a form of control. Consider this: if you enjoy giving or doing things for others but resist allowing others to do the same for you, you're exerting control over them. By doing so, you prevent them from experiencing the joy of giving to you. Consequently, you close yourself off to receiving in various forms, such as assistance, clients, financial support, or love. This control mechanism acts as a barrier, hindering you from attaining the things you desire most. We'll delve deeper into this topic later on.

One of the most significant disguises we wear is the one we present to ourselves. No one deceives us more than we deceive ourselves. Donning the mask of who we think we should be, rather than embracing and fully owning all aspects of ourselves, is draining. This behavior only fuels our control issues and undermines our potential as successful leaders and entrepreneurs. Concealing our true, authentic selves often stems from childhood experiences where being genuine was not accepted. This is especially true for individuals somewhere on the neurodivergent spectrum, exhibiting symptoms or diagnoses such as ADD, ADHD, HSP, ASD, BPD, or PTSD, among others. It's essential to remember that these labels don't define us; instead, the symptoms or conditions can be viewed as superpowers that significantly contribute to our potential to raise our ceiling and achieve success.

What you may have perceived as high performance is actually high-functioning. The very source of your superpowers can also be the root of your self-sabotage. This means that those same gifts and habits can keep your lowest points lower and widen the gap between your highest achievements and deepest struggles. It's why even the most accomplished individuals can face significant internal battles and why entrepreneurs often feel isolated and disconnected from others. This dynamic is also why Impostor Syndrome frequently rears its head at every stage of success and entrepreneurship. Personally, I view Impostor Syndrome as a positive sign because it indicates that you're taking action and striving for significant achievements. The real issue lies in the misalignment between what you think or believe about yourself and reality. It serves as a messenger, highlighting areas that need attention and reminding you that you have complete control over your beliefs, narratives, and thought patterns.

Source

Your Toolkit

You aren't born with a toolkit; it's something you develop over time, consisting of coping mechanisms, mindset, beliefs, and habits that evolve throughout your life. Much of this toolkit is acquired from your family during your formative years, with the bulk of learning happening before the age of seven. Consequently, many of the patterns and traumas you carry into adulthood are rooted in these early familial experiences. Often, your family members themselves are unaware of the behaviors and traits they pass down (which can be incredibly frustrating). This foundational toolkit establishes your baseline, shaping the minimum standards you're willing to accept in various aspects of your life. For instance, if you grew up with emotionally unavailable parents, you're likely to tolerate emotional unavailability in your relationships (your floor), even if you aspire to deeper emotional connections (your ceiling).

When your toolkit lacks the necessary components to consistently reach your goals and elevate your potential, it indicates a shaky foundation. This is why you may find yourself grappling with self-doubt and inconsistency—your existing tools and habits may be more of a hindrance than a help. For instance, in my case, my toolkit was missing crucial coping skills to navigate emotions like hurt, disappointment, or rejection effectively. Instead of seeking support from loved ones or processing my feelings through journaling, I resorted to stuffing my emotions with food and distracting myself from them. While these may be considered coping mechanisms, they are ultimately unhealthy ones. Although they provided temporary relief, they led to significant long-term issues for me.

I found myself resorting to self-soothing techniques to alleviate immediate discomfort rather than confronting and learning from it. This reliance on instant gratification often proves challenging to overcome, despite the fact that your ability to delay gratification is a significant predictor of long-term success. Maintaining focus can be arduous and uncomfortable, prompting you to seek solace in distractions, particularly when activities like checking social media or responding to emails offer quick dopamine boosts. Essentially, you're using these distractions to ease the discomfort of concentration. Similarly, engaging in difficult conversations with your partner or cultivating emotional intimacy requires effort, even if you genuinely desire it. Consequently, it's often more tempting to bury yourself in work and prioritize productivity. These methods of self-soothing discomfort are indicative of your current threshold in action. Recognizing and acknowledging this pattern is crucial for initiating change.

This isn't about passing judgment on the toolkit you currently possess or the individuals from whom you acquired it. It's essential to honor yourself and acknowledge that your present toolkit has brought you to where you are today! Recognizing what isn't serving you and realizing the need to acquire new skills to elevate your baseline is a significant step forward, and you're here because you're prepared to embrace change!

When your toolkit lacks the necessary tools to raise your standards effectively, it results in a shaky and insecure foundation, akin to a Jenga tower on the verge of collapse. The instability inherent in this weak base contributes to various control issues and prompts us to maintain a carefully curated facade for others. Striving to embody what we believe others expect from us becomes a coping mechanism to conceal this shaky foundation. However, this instability breeds fear, scarcity, and a pervasive sense of being out of control.

Many of the choices you're making stem from the fear of losing the perceived safety and stability you've established in your life. However, this stability is primarily an external condition and, as such, doesn't address the underlying issue. The root of the instability lies within, and no external circumstance can fully resolve it. Consequently, decisions are often guided by a desire to preserve this sense of safety and stability or to avoid discomfort, such as hesitating to leave your current job to pursue your own business, remaining in a job for the benefits it provides, or staying in unhealthy relationships well past their expiration date. Any of these changes would disrupt the perceived safety and stability because they lie outside your comfort zone.

Entrepreneurship, as you may have noticed, is inherently uncertain and uncomfortable, triggering your stress response on a daily basis as you navigate its challenges. This constant triggering leads to instinctual reactions like fight, flight, freeze, or fawn, as well as the self-soothing behaviors mentioned earlier that help you cope with the chaos. The innate need for safety and stability often takes precedence over motivation and long-term goals, influencing decisions in ways that prioritize comfort over growth.

Floor Vs. Ceiling

Success or failure hinges entirely on your standards. Your "ceiling" represents your maximum potential for success, encompassing not just your loftiest aspirations but also what you're presently capable of achieving under optimal circumstances. By daring to dream bigger and setting loftier goals, you effectively raise and expand your ceiling, envisioning possibilities like increased wealth, a larger home, or a nicer car than what you currently possess. This expansion renders your ceiling boundless.

Conversely, your "floor" signifies your baseline standard, the lowest level you're willing to accept. True progress is anchored in your floor, as it serves as the default setting that shapes your daily actions and yields the most tangible outcomes. It represents the minimum threshold of acceptability rather than mere desire.

You've likely encountered tales of lottery winners who squandered their fortunes or celebrities and athletes who faced bankruptcy despite their substantial earnings. In each case, these individuals experienced a significant increase in their ceiling—often rapidly—but failed to fortify their financial floor through diligent effort. Their lowest acceptable standard remained one of financial instability or significantly lower income than their maximum potential. For one person, feeling financially strapped might kick in when their monthly earnings dip to $100,000, while another may experience it when their bank account hits overdraft.

Often, individuals concentrate solely on elevating their ceiling, which may be the case for you in your life and business right now. You're likely envisioning all the aspirations, dreams, and goals you wish to achieve, along with the necessary steps like marketing, sales, and systems to support those ambitions. But have you ever considered your floor? What are the minimum standards you currently tolerate that should be elevated to aid you in reaching your goals? It's crucial to scrutinize your daily habits and routines, especially the subconscious ones, to determine if they're contributing positively or hindering your success. For instance, compare gratitude journaling with starting your day by watching the news or scrolling through social media. Certain actions are more conducive to nurturing the right mindset and energy for the day.

Expanding the disparity between your ceiling and floor is akin to the adage, "One step forward, two steps back." Achieving a new milestone or success elevates your ceiling. However, if you neglect to raise your floor, your minimum standard, the gap widens. Consequently, reverting to your lowest standard may feel like regressing even further. This underscores the significance of raising your floor, which, in reality, facilitates the elevation of your ceiling. Maintaining a narrower gap ensures that your progress remains steady over time, making it a pivotal factor for sustained success.

Compartmentalizing

Another aspect of maintaining a low floor and lacking stability in your foundation is through compartmentalization and the omission of painful experiences and histories you'd rather not confront. This includes aspects you dislike about yourself, unresolved anger and resentment, and any truths you're avoiding. It becomes a learned behavior to lock away these hurts, failures, rejections, and self-loathing sentiments in separate compartments, hidden from the world and even from yourself. This habit fosters self-rejection and denies the validity of your shadow side, which comprises facets of yourself you keep concealed. However, acknowledging and integrating these aspects is crucial for raising your floor and mitigating self-sabotage tendencies. For instance, while my light side readily expresses emotions and empathy, my shadow side involves initiating action, which necessitates conscious effort. Recognizing these dynamics isn't about labeling them as "bad," but rather about fostering awareness and implementing strategies to elevate your baseline and diminish self-sabotage patterns.

However, that shadow side inevitably manifests itself through sporadic, intrusive thoughts that surface during moments of solitude, such as when driving alone or trying to fall asleep, or when your inner rebel begins to act out. These are the thoughts and emotions you instinctively try to sidestep, distracting yourself with busyness or seeking solace in social media. It's the reason you shy away from being alone or embracing stillness—to evade confronting those unsettling feelings. It's essential to differentiate between reacting to these emotions and genuinely experiencing them.

Whether you embrace it or not, all those aspects are integral parts of you, even if you choose to overlook them. The more you attempt to push away the pain and darkness, trying to erase them from your being, the more disconnected you become from your authentic self. You can't be truly whole when you excise parts of yourself. Instead, you fill that void with busyness, relationships, food, alcohol, distractions, exercise, and anything else that helps you evade facing the truth of who you are, shadows included. Yet, therein lies your truth and power: within the personal history you've been trying to deny, the thoughts and emotions that evoke guilt and shame, and amidst the anger, pain, and resentment.

The only path to constructing a solid, enduring foundation is by confronting all aspects of yourself. However, the crucial element is to do so constructively rather than destructively, in a manner that is both safe and effective. This approach is essential for elevating your lowest standard and setting higher benchmarks for success. Your true strength lies in embracing not just the light within you but also your darkness and pain. It's this depth of experience that enables you to empathize and connect deeply with others. Embracing your full spectrum allows you to craft an authentic personal brand, become a transformative leader, excel as a partner, and achieve significant financial goals. In essence, it's your ability to confront your darkness that allows your brightest qualities to shine forth, as it is the wellspring of your greatest strength.

SOLUTION

Systems

Frederick Alexander, founder of the Alexander Technique, said, "People do not decide their futures, they decide their habits and their habits decide their futures." Your goal represents your desired outcome, while your system comprises the array of daily habits designed to achieve it. Success hinges on the effectiveness of your systems, which either maintain or elevate your minimum standard to support the expansion of your maximum potential. The process of fortifying a sturdy foundation lies not merely in awareness but in the consistent actions you undertake. Establishing daily routines necessitates systems, both personally and in your business endeavors. By implementing numerous systems, success becomes more attainable, as you conserve mental energy that would otherwise be spent recalling tasks or exerting effort to fulfill them. Moreover, you evade self-criticism and regret for failing to execute intended actions. Systems empower you to elevate your standards and resist reverting to the old habits associated with your former minimum standard.

Keep your systems simple! Their purpose is to streamline difficult tasks, not to induce overthinking or analysis paralysis. The more complicated you make your systems, the more likely you are to remain stagnant. For instance, if you aim to establish a morning workout routine, pinpoint the earliest stage in your habitual cycle where you typically encounter excuses or self-sabotage, and then devise a system to counteract them. A typical system might involve preparing the night before by laying out your workout clothes and shoes, setting an additional alarm that requires you to get out of bed to silence it, and programming your coffee maker to start brewing just before you wake up. This system ensures you're primed for success before your self-sabotage tendencies kick in, thereby lowering the barrier to follow-through and making success more attainable, even when initiating uncomfortable changes.

My favorite systems are those I can set and forget, sparing me the effort of remembering to execute a bunch of tasks. For instance, our CRM (customer relationship management system) includes built-in automation features that handle follow-ups with new leads and connections, as well as maintaining contact after sales or demo calls. Additionally, I've configured alarms on my smartwatch to sound at regular intervals when I typically become distracted or lose focus during my routines, helping me to stay on task. The most effective systems often involve eliminating triggers altogether. For example, if you want to avoid checking your phone first thing in the morning, simply keep it stored elsewhere in the house, away from your bedroom. It's as straightforward as that!

FOUNDATION

Success hinges on a sturdy foundation, and if this chapter is resonating with you, it's likely because your foundation needs strengthening, much like many others. As someone who's also on the path of recovery from being a high-achiever and perfectionist, I understand the tendency to leap to step 27 before completing steps 2, 3, and 4. If your foundation is rooted in unhealthy family patterns, generational traumas, personal trauma or instability, failure, limiting beliefs, disconnect, and doubt, then these issues will manifest as control issues and high-functioning behavior. Eventually, they'll lead to burnout and increased stress, more frequent sabotage behaviors, and inconsistency in business, cash flow, and relationships. Consider this example as illustrating what you're doing with the information shared in this chapter. You're delving into your foundation, addressing the root issues compromising its integrity, and constructing a new foundation for your success with improved systems. You'll unearth and clear out the clutter, patch holes and weak spots, and establish a robust base to realize the life and business of your dreams.

The cornerstone of your foundation is a robust connection with yourself. It's simple yet profound because it encompasses everything. This connection forms the bedrock of your confidence, authenticity, aligned goals, and actions. It's the journey toward embracing every aspect of yourself and loving yourself as a whole, without compartmentalization. Building this connection entails self-management—taking control of yourself and ceasing to expend time, energy, and emotion on matters beyond your control. Reclaiming your power is crucial to forging this connection. Failure to do so will result in the unresolved issues you're avoiding surfacing in your relationships, business, employees, systems, and health. This was my experience, and it's what I've been assisting entrepreneurs with for over a decade—addressing the root of their business problems, which often lies within themselves. No more chasing strategies to superficially alleviate symptoms like inconsistent revenue, ineffective marketing, or low sales conversions.

The journey of self-empowerment and laying the groundwork for success begins with the implementation of my Aligned Abundance Process™. This methodology forms the heart of my bestselling book, *Be a Boss & Fire That Bitch*, where I meticulously explore each step. Named the "Aligned Abundance Process," it guides you through the process of establishing a profound connection with your authentic self, rather than conforming to societal expectations of success. As you find fulfillment and a sense of sufficiency in this state of alignment—the wellspring of abundance—you begin to manifest and attract greater opportunities in your life and business. This process serves as the gateway to unlocking abundance, prosperity, and wealth across various facets of your life, including health, relationships, business, and beyond. Ultimately, it empowers you to confidently and authentically express yourself, illuminating the world with your unique gifts and talents.

💡 Actionable Tips

Aligned Abundance Process

This five-step signature process stems from my personal journey of trauma and addiction recovery. It stands as the pivotal factor in reclaiming control over myself and my ADHD, lifting both my floor and ceiling, and orchestrating significant transformations in my life. Through this process, I managed to overhaul my health, shedding half my body weight and freeing myself from all medications. Moreover, it played a crucial role in nurturing my enduring marriage of over two decades and in establishing multiple seven-figure companies. By diligently following these steps daily, I've cultivated the consistency needed to elevate my standards and navigate through challenges without succumbing to distractions. This disciplined approach instills the confidence necessary to propel you toward your aspirations, sparing you the exhaustive cycle of pushing and hustling only to undermine your own success.

ANCHOR YOUR ROUTINES – Consistently engaging in daily actions to prioritize yourself, fostering a deeper connection and elevating your baseline. The essence lies in integrating straightforward activities that cater to your physical, intellectual, emotional, and spiritual well-being, as they inherently influence other facets of your life—financially, socially, and environmentally. This sustained commitment fosters a sense of trust in yourself, ultimately fostering trust, equilibrium, and reliability in other aspects of your life.

System

- Set up a daily habit tracker, whether it's on paper or digital, to help you stay accountable and recognize your behavioral patterns. Monitor activities such as expressing gratitude, celebrating victories, engaging in physical activity, reading, and any other habits that contribute to your overall well-being.
- Observe patterns of avoidance or inconsistency without judgment or attaching significance to them. Recognize areas where you can tweak your habits and behaviors to achieve the results you desire.

RELEASE YOUR BAGGAGE – Release the thoughts, emotions, and limiting narratives that prompt reactive behavior, and relinquish control over things beyond your influence. It's essential to vent constructively, preventing self-sabotage or outbursts on others. The weight of burdens and baggage acts as anchors, hindering your progress even when you're giving your all. Embrace the lessons, then release what no longer serves you.

System

- Incorporate a tool or technique to release emotional baggage and regulate your nervous system, breaking the cycle of triggers and stress. Begin by practicing your chosen technique daily for a few minutes, focusing on your current feelings about recent events. This regular practice builds familiarity with the tool and minimizes avoidance of addressing significant or longstanding issues.
- EFT (Tapping), Breathwork, Write & Burn, and bullet journaling are a few examples.

RESPECT YOUR BOUNDARIES – Establishing boundaries involves taking ownership of yourself and your aspirations while fostering inner security and consistency. Directing your attention solely towards what you have control over alleviates worry, anxiety, and much of the stress. Conversely, fixating on uncontrollable aspects tends to fuel feelings of powerlessness and triggers self-sabotage tendencies. Remember, you cannot dictate others' actions or outcomes, only your own decisions and boundaries. It's crucial to prioritize your own well-being: your time, energy, physical and emotional health, aspirations, and personal boundaries. By valuing these aspects of yourself, you set the stage for others to do the same.

System

- Time management is frequently at the forefront of boundary-setting challenges and serves as an excellent starting point. Begin by establishing designated time blocks for client meetings, networking, or team collaboration sessions, and integrate them into an online

calendar booking system. This allows individuals to schedule appointments based on your predetermined availability, promoting efficient use of your time while respecting your boundaries.
- Establish systems and designated time blocks for focusing on various aspects of your life, including personal growth, nurturing relationships, supporting your team, and enhancing your business.

BE OPEN TO RECEIVE – Finally, grant yourself permission to embrace success and welcome the abundance that you've been tirelessly pursuing but inadvertently blocking. Remember, success is not achieved in isolation! You need not shoulder the burden alone. The relentless hustle, driven by a desire to control outcomes, only serves to hinder your progress. It leads to burnout, business setbacks, and potential impacts on your health and relationships. Be receptive to assistance from your network, collaborative efforts, your team, partner, family, and beyond. Most importantly, allow yourself to receive what you desire with confidence, knowing unequivocally that you are worthy and deserving of success, even if it unfolds effortlessly.

System

- The simplest system is to challenge yourself to ask for help or delegate a task every day.
- Just say "Thank you" when receiving a compliment or positive feedback without deflecting or diminishing it.

RAISE YOUR STANDARDS – Upgrade and elevate how you show up, what you use, and who you surround yourself with to consistently be your best. This requires honest evaluation. Identify your current standards for yourself, your life, relationships, and business, then focus on raising them.

Clearly define the minimum standards your future successful self will have. What are they eating, reading, and doing regularly? Who are they spending time with? How are you showing up for yourself, your relationships, and your business? Dive deep to identify the standards that need improvement.

System

- Review your current self-management standards through the lens of the previous four steps: habits and routines; time, energy, and relationships (boundaries); emotion management and reactivity (self-soothing); and receiving help or what you want. Aim to raise the floor for each area by making just one change to improve in each aspect. Implement these changes daily until you observe progress, then add more adjustments to further elevate your standards.
- Another effective system involves transforming apology moments into gratitude moments. Instead of apologizing, which centers the attention on yourself, shift the focus to the other person by expressing gratitude instead.
  - I'm sorry I'm late. → Thank you for your patience.
  - I'm sorry I have to reschedule. → Thank you for your flexibility.

Connect

If you'd like to go deeper into the concepts in this chapter, grab a copy of my bestselling book, *Be a Boss & Fire That Bitch: Quiet Your Inner Critic & Finally Believe You're GOOD ENOUGH.* Available on Amazon or go to firethatbitchbook.com.

Additionally, I've also created a free tool and resource to support each of these steps shared here, grab them at: firethatbitchbook.com/resources.

If what I shared in this chapter resonated with you, let's connect!

Here are a few ways to learn more about my business systems, leadership and strategic consulting, courses, and coaching programs to ensure your success.

- stacyraske.com
- beinflowential.com
- Facebook Community: www.facebook.com/groups/stacyraske
- Follow me and connect on all socials: @stacyraske
- Facebook, Instagram, LinkedIn, YouTube, and beyond

ABOUT THE AUTHOR

Stacy Raske is a bestselling author, speaker, peak performance coach, energy optimization specialist, executive coach, leadership expert, business and systems strategist, and Iraq War Veteran. She helps disruptive leaders and organizations implement systems and strategies to elevate performance, people, and profit. She empowers impact-driven leaders to embrace their inner rebel and leverage their genius to disrupt the status quo.

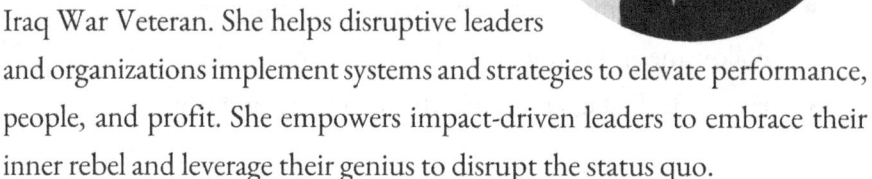

Her mission in life is to unlock the highest potential in others by shattering the invisible ceiling and fully living their purpose while enjoying the ride. Stacy has written for and been featured in numerous magazines, including Authority Magazine, Yahoo Finance, and Business Insider.

Using the toolkit she's learned during her trauma and addiction recovery, she's mentored and inspired thousands with her vulnerability, authenticity, and impactful storytelling. Stacy believes that "everything we need to be successful is already within us and we must give ourselves permission to embody all we desire."

She lives outside Tampa, Florida with her husband, Jeffry, two fabulous motorcycles, and two cats.

CHAPTER 5

Two Years in the Digital Marketing Trenches:

How Mastery Paves the Way to Business Success

by Joseph Compton

📝 The Story

"You'll need to sign the papers now or the unit will be given to the next person in line."

We knew our lives were about to drastically change.

As the sun set on a typical day in Huntsville, Alabama, my wife Brittany and I sat in our modest apartment, contemplating the latest twist in our journey. Brittany had left her home in New Mexico to be with me, and while our love was strong, blending our families hadn't been easy. Her 11-year-old son and my 6-year-old brought joy and challenges in equal measure.

After yet another failed attempt at launching a home business, we found ourselves entrenched in the grind of long hours at a Toyota dealership, scraping by to make ends meet. I hustled on the car lot, braving the elements to greet every "up" with a smile, while Brittany toiled away in the service department.

Then came the news that would change everything: we were expecting our first child together. Amidst the joy, a shadow of worry crept in. How could we sustain our hectic schedules with a newborn in tow? We knew we needed help, so we started exploring the idea of moving closer to family.

Chattanooga, Tennessee, seemed like the answer—a community with affordable housing and familial support. We applied for a townhouse, thinking we had time to plan. But fate had other ideas. Just a week later, a call came—there was a unit available, but we had to act fast.

With a mix of excitement and trepidation, we made the decision to leap into the unknown. Before we even arrived in Chattanooga, reality set in. I hadn't found a job yet, but my passion for digital marketing and sales funnels burned bright. Despite two years of setbacks and self-doubt, I couldn't shake the dream of making it my career.

Then, just as we prepared for the move, an opportunity emerged—a job in digital marketing, the field I longed to enter. It was decision time: settle for another dealership job or chase my dream. With Brittany's unwavering support, we took a leap of faith, quitting our jobs and moving to Chattanooga.

The months that followed were a rollercoaster. I poured my heart and soul into online communities, hoping to catch a break. But success proved elusive, and with bills mounting, the pressure was on. Yet, with each setback, I persisted, driven by a determination to provide for my growing family.

Then, just when it seemed like all hope was lost, a breakthrough came. With the helping hand of my friend Tod Holland, I landed the job at the internet marketing company I'd been dreaming of—a testament to the power of perseverance and the unwavering support of friends.

But our journey didn't end there. As we settled into our new life in Chattanooga, we faced fresh challenges and triumphs. From late nights building sales funnels to moments of celebration with our expanding family, every step brought us closer to our dreams.

Looking back, it's clear that signing those lease papers was more than just a decision—it was a turning point. It was the moment we embraced uncertainty and embraced the possibility of a brighter future. And as we continue to chase our dreams and build our lives together, we carry that spirit of resilience and hope with us, knowing that no matter what challenges lie ahead, we'll face them together, as a family.

🎯 The Principle

Reflecting on our journey, I realized that daily practice, consistent value delivery, and unwavering persistence were the cornerstones of reaching the next step in my career.

For two years, I immersed myself in the world of digital marketing, honing my skills and expanding my knowledge. Each day brought new challenges and opportunities to learn, but I remained steadfast in my commitment to mastery.

Through relentless practice and dedication, I gradually elevated my expertise, inching closer to my desired destination with each passing day. Whether it was refining my understanding of sales funnels or mastering the intricacies of online community engagement, I embraced the grind, knowing that greatness is forged through perseverance.

But practice alone wasn't enough. Alongside my daily efforts, I prioritized delivering value to others. In online communities and forums, I shared insights, offered assistance, and provided actionable advice, all with the aim of making a meaningful impact.

By consistently adding value to the lives of others, I not only established myself as a trusted authority but also cultivated a network of supporters and allies who championed my journey. It was a reminder that success isn't achieved in isolation but through meaningful connections and genuine contributions to the community.

And perhaps most importantly, I refused to succumb to the allure of defeat. Despite the setbacks and challenges that inevitably arose, I remained resolute in my pursuit of success. Whether faced with rejection, financial strain, or self-doubt, I refused to let adversity dictate my future.

Instead, I embraced each obstacle as an opportunity to grow stronger and more resilient. Every setback served as a lesson, guiding me toward greater clarity and purpose in my journey.

In the end, it was this unwavering commitment to practice, value, and persistence that propelled me forward. It wasn't easy, and there were moments when the path ahead seemed daunting. But by staying true to my principles and remaining steadfast in my pursuit of excellence, I ultimately reached the pinnacle of success—a testament to the transformative power of resilience and perseverance.

Actionable Tips

You've heard me talk a lot about sales funnels, and you may be asking yourself, "What the heck is a sales funnel?"

Imagine a sales funnel as a sequence of interconnected web pages designed to guide your ideal prospect through a sales journey. This process aims to introduce them to you before a sales call or to facilitate a purchase decision directly within the funnel.

Funnels can be used for many different goals, such as lead generation, promoting events, selling products, scheduling appointments, and much more.

If you're new to digital marketing or seeking to enhance your lead generation efforts, I'd like to share my fundamental blueprint for generating leads at *no cost* using social media.

After years of studying and practice, I've identified a proven 5-step framework:

1. **Define Your Audience:** Get crystal clear on who your ideal customers are. Analyze their demographics, challenges, goals, and interests. The more specifically you can define them, the better.
2. **Create Irresistible Free Offers/Lead Magnets:** Develop free educational resources like ebooks, courses, or toolkits that provide real value to your audience. This is the bait to attract your ideal prospects.
3. **Build Effective Lead Funnels:** Create simple lead generation funnels that deliver your lead magnets in exchange for the visitor's contact information. This is where you collect leads.
4. **Promote Through Targeted Outreach:** Write social media posts centered around your lead magnets. Ask your audience if they want access to your free resource and to comment on your post if they do. Send the link to your lead funnel to each person who comments via direct message (DM). This process will help you build your email list.
5. **Optimize and Repeat:** Analyze data and feedback to identify what's working and what's not. Refine each stage of the process, then repeat for continuous improvement.

This 5-step system allows you to methodically turn your knowledge into income by providing real value. The key is relentlessly fine-tuning each step of the process based on data and customer feedback.

If you follow this framework and continuously optimize it, you'll be able to generate predictable lead flow and scale your business. Feel free to join my Facebook group or check out my ebook (each listed below) for more details!

Connect

Ready to take your digital marketing game to the next level? Join the Sales Funnel Fanatics Facebook Group for invaluable insights and community support. Plus, grab your copy of the free eBook, The Sales Funnel Fanatics Resource Cheat Sheet, packed with actionable tips and strategies to optimize your sales funnels. Elevate your business with expert guidance and resources—let's make your digital marketing endeavors a resounding success together! Claim your free guide now at:

josephbcompton.com/freeguide.

ABOUT THE AUTHOR

Hey there, I'm Joseph, and I've been navigating the digital marketing realm since 2019. With over a decade of experience in sales under my belt, I've honed my skills to help small businesses thrive in the online landscape. Passionate about sharing knowledge and empowering others, I find joy in teaching and supporting individuals as they reach their business and life goals. Ready to elevate your business to new heights? Let's collaborate and make your vision a reality. Whether you're looking to streamline your sales funnels or enhance your online presence, count on me to be your trusted guide. Let's take your business to the next level together.

CHAPTER 6

The Power of Connection:

Creating a Positive Work Environment

by David Oltman

📝 The Story

It was March 15th, 2017, a significant day for me as I had just been promoted from an entry-level position to the role of operations manager at the transportation company where I worked. Under the guidance of one of the best bosses I'd ever encountered, I found myself in a new realm of responsibility. What set him apart was his exceptional clarity in expectations and communication. He had a knack for demonstrating the intricacies of the job and then empowering his team to execute tasks in a manner that best suited their individual talents.

One of his most remarkable qualities was his ability to grant autonomy within roles, allowing employees to leverage their strengths while ensuring alignment with the overall objectives. His method involved regular reviews to refine approaches and foster personal growth, a practice at which he excelled.

Moreover, he instilled a standard for managers to engage with entry-level employees, fostering an environment that not only promoted teamwork but also nurtured friendships. Managers were encouraged to glean three to five new insights daily from trainees, fostering a culture of continuous learning and collaboration among the management team.

The nature of the job itself was demanding, characterized by high performance expectations and inherent stress due to the urgency of loading packages onto delivery vehicles promptly and efficiently. Maintaining a steady pace and operational efficiency were paramount, adding to the pressure of ensuring seamless operations.

Amidst the established operational standards, Jim, the boss in question, went above and beyond, setting additional benchmarks that not only maintained operational efficiency but also fostered a vibrant and enjoyable work environment. Working under Jim's leadership was truly one of the most rewarding experiences of my managerial career. Our shared vision on how to treat people and manage operations made it an ideal learning environment.

During my two-year tenure as an operations manager under Jim's guidance, I had the opportunity to cultivate several teams to a level of self-sufficiency. One notable achievement was the transformation of a highly demanding area within the facility. I expanded the team from a small group to a robust unit of twelve individuals, completely overhauling the workspace to enhance safety and efficiency. By implementing rigorous communication and training standards, I not only fostered strong bonds among team members but also ensured that each member possessed a deep understanding of their role, enabling them to advance into leadership roles within the company.

However, despite the fulfilling experience under Jim's leadership, a major life event marked a turning point, leading me to encounter a vastly different leadership style. Transitioning to a large transportation corporation introduced me to a new boss and an entirely new set of challenges. On March 5th, 2019, following a full shift at the transportation company, I embarked on another stint as a pool cleaner, unaware of the events that would transpire.

Upon returning home, I was greeted by my wife and our daughter, who was our only child at that time. With a second child on the way, our household was bustling with anticipation. Despite the busyness, I had to prioritize my college coursework, juggling a demanding load of eight college credits alongside my responsibilities at home. My wife, a dedicated stay-at-home mom, was simultaneously completing her nursing degree while caring for our daughter, leaving me to handle the remaining household duties.

Before delving further into this chapter of my life, it's important to provide some context. I have a younger brother who served in the Marine Corps Reserves. Recently married, he volunteered for a deployment to Kuwait, preceded by a month-long training in California alongside his assigned unit. Following his return home for a brief 10-day leave, we welcomed a new addition to our family in the form of my sister-in-law.

On March 4th, a Monday, which marked my brother's third day back from his deployment preparation, we took the opportunity to visit our grandfather at the nursing home where he resided. After spending quality time with him, we treated ourselves to a delightful lunch at a charming restaurant in Maple Plain, not far from the nursing home.

We decided to grab lunch at McGarry's Irish Pub, a cozy spot where we unexpectedly bumped into my uncle, who happened to be visiting my grandfather as well. Coincidentally, McGarry's was one of my uncle's clients, so we all enjoyed a meal together. After lunch, my brother and I headed home, cherishing the time we had left together before his year-long deployment.

As the afternoon waned, my brother embarked on a snowmobile ride home, eager to take advantage of the abundant snowfall that March. The following day, he and a couple of friends planned a two-day trip to a casino in Hinckley. Little did I know, March 5th, 2019, would forever alter the course of my life.

I received a call around 3:21 PM while I was catching up on homework after finishing both of my jobs. It was his best friend, delivering devastating news of a tragic accident. My brother had collided with a flatbed tow truck, resulting in his untimely death. The sudden loss of my dear brother, whom I shared a close bond with, left me shattered.

In the aftermath, I took advantage of the bereavement leave provided by my employer and devoted myself to supporting my newly widowed sister-in-law. Despite the brief duration of their marriage—only 33 days—I helped her navigate the painful process of planning his funeral.

So, during the week of funeral planning, I barely managed to squeeze in a total of 14 hours of sleep. After those seven days elapsed—five days paid leave, plus the weekend—I returned to work. Except, I didn't return on schedule. My body had reached its limits; I needed time to process not just mentally, but physically too.

I attempted to catch up on sleep, hitting the hay around 6:00 PM on March 12th, with my managerial duties starting at midnight. I anticipated a solid six hours of rest, but I was out like a light, impervious to any alarms. It wasn't until 6:00 AM the following morning that I stirred, realizing I had slept through my shift. I promptly called in, acknowledging my absence. The next day, I made an effort to show up, but I struggled to function and ended up leaving after just half a day.

Fast forward to March 15th, roughly 10 days since my brother's passing. I found myself summoned to the office of a manager three levels above me. While I had a strong rapport with my immediate superiors, my relationship with this higher-level manager was more distant. Seated in his office, he endeavored to connect with me, sharing a deeply personal story of loss—a gesture aimed at providing perspective and support during this challenging time. Out of respect for his privacy, I won't delve into the specifics of his narrative.

He shared his story with me, aiming to spur me back into action. However, the delivery felt more like a blunt directive: "Life throws curveballs, now get back to work." It struck me that he had lost sight of the importance of employee well-being, a stark contrast to my first boss who prioritized fostering a positive environment amid workplace pressures.

The Principle

While my good boss cultivated a supportive atmosphere, the bad boss seemed to exacerbate stress, particularly during this trying period in my life. Alone in his office, his words revealed the organizational dynamics from the top down. It became clear that while my immediate supervisor advocated for positive change, those higher up prioritized outcomes over the human element.

As business owners, it's imperative to acknowledge that our employees and clients are the backbone of our enterprise. Neglecting their well-being risks driving them away, as people ultimately quit people, not companies. Therefore, it's essential for business owners to empathize with individuals, understand their challenges, and foster an environment where they can thrive, even amidst adversity.

Building connections and establishing relationships with employees can set you apart not just as a business owner, but as a leader. By understanding their needs and supporting them through challenges, you cultivate loyalty to both you and your vision. Ultimately, having a loyal and invested workforce is invaluable for the success of any enterprise.

Actionable Tips

In today's business world, taking care of your team and building strong connections with both employees and clients is key to lasting success. As a business owner, it's important to create a supportive environment, understand individual challenges, and form meaningful relationships. Here are three practical tips you can take to create a positive workplace, foster loyalty among your team, and improve client relationships.

1. **Prioritize a Supportive Atmosphere:** Take proactive steps to cultivate a supportive atmosphere within your organization. This involves creating an environment where employees feel valued, heard, and supported. Encourage open communication, provide resources for personal and professional development, and actively address any sources of stress or conflict in the workplace. By prioritizing the well-being of your team members, you can foster a positive work environment that enhances productivity and employee satisfaction.
2. **Empathize and Understand Challenges:** As a business owner, it's crucial to empathize with your employees and understand the challenges they may be facing. Take the time to listen to their concerns, seek feedback on their experiences within the organization, and offer support where needed. By demonstrating empathy and understanding, you can build trust and rapport with your team members, leading to stronger relationships and increased loyalty to the company.
3. **Invest in Relationship Building:** Focus on building meaningful connections and relationships with your employees. Take the initiative to get to know them on a personal level, understand their

individual strengths and aspirations, and actively engage in mentorship and coaching opportunities. By investing in relationship building, you can create a sense of belonging and camaraderie within your team, fostering a positive and supportive work culture. Additionally, prioritize relationship building with clients by understanding their needs, providing exceptional service, and maintaining open lines of communication. This will not only strengthen client loyalty but also contribute to the long-term success of your business.

Connect

Ensuring the welfare of your business and employees is paramount. This includes having someone to oversee operations and ensure continuity, regardless of circumstances. If you're a business owner seeking guidance in this area, you can connect with me on Facebook (Clarity Insurance) or visit clarityinsuranceteam.com to schedule a consultation. Let's ensure everything works seamlessly according to your vision.

ABOUT THE AUTHOR

David is a devoted family man who treasures his role as a caring husband and father to two incredible children. His top priority is creating memorable moments and fostering growth and joy with his kids through various activities. When not enjoying family time, David is dedicated to assisting homeowners and business owners in optimizing their financial and insurance plans. His unwavering commitment to both his family and clients showcases his compassionate and determined character. With a multifaceted approach to life, David embodies a deep dedication to personal and professional fulfillment, striving for success in every aspect of his journey.

CHAPTER 7
Cultivating a Sales-Driven Culture
by Ben Ludwig

📝 The Story

When sales comes to mind, many envision high-pressure tactics, pushy car salesmen, and the infamous "talk to my manager" maneuver. It's no wonder that for most, the term "salesperson" is met with skepticism. Time is precious, and the last thing anyone wants is to feel manipulated into a purchase they didn't truly want or need.

But why has sales acquired such a negative connotation in our culture? Why can't sales be about genuinely helping people make informed decisions that benefit them? Take the fitness industry, for example. Shouldn't every fitness professional be eager to share their products and services, knowing they have the potential to transform lives for the better?

The truth is, the art of sales has been tarnished by those who prioritize profit over people. The relentless pursuit of an extra dollar has led to a landscape where genuine, ethical salesmanship is a rarity. And in this climate, truly skilled salespeople are few and far between.

A couple of years back, there was a knock at my door on a lazy Saturday evening. Now, I'm no stranger to the world of sales, so when I saw a young salesman standing there, I couldn't help but admire his hustle. Despite the temptation to send him on his way, I decided to let him in.

After all, I've had my fair share of sales pitches, and I enjoy seeing how well they can play the game.

As he launched into his spiel about "done-for-you" pest control, I decided to give him a bit of a test. I dropped a few subtle hints about my interest in the service, just to see if he'd pick up on them. But instead of launching into a rehearsed pitch, he surprised me. He started a conversation, asking about my job, my family, and even my hobbies.

I have to admit, I was impressed. Here was a young guy who understood the power of building a genuine connection. He didn't bombard me with facts and figures or try to pressure me into making a decision. Instead, he took the time to get to know me, to understand my needs and concerns.

As we chatted, he gradually steered the conversation back to pest control, but it felt natural, like we were just two neighbors having a chat over the fence. By the time he finally got around to talking about his product, I was already sold. Not because of some fancy sales pitch or flashy guarantee, but because he had taken the time to listen and to genuinely engage with me.

In the end, I signed up for the service, not because I felt pressured or manipulated, but because I genuinely believed it was the right choice for me and my family. And it was all thanks to that young salesman who understood that sometimes, the best way to make a sale is to simply have a conversation.

🎯 The Principle

You know what really struck a chord with me? It was how that young salesman understood the value of time, our most precious asset. He looked at me and said, "Mr. Ludwig, it seems like you've got a lot on your plate –

between your businesses and your family. Our product could help ease that load, giving you more time for what truly matters."

Now, that's what I call effective salesmanship. And here's the thing: becoming a great salesperson doesn't always require the traits you might expect. So, if you're not a natural public speaker, you don't ooze charisma, or you haven't mastered the art of "selling ice to an eskimo," don't let that deter you. In fact, I encourage you to lean in and discover the principles that can truly elevate your sales game.

Principle 1: Mindset

Alright, here's a confession: I'm an Android user. Now, before all you Apple aficionados tune out, hear me out. It's pretty comical, actually – almost everyone in my circle, from friends and family to coworkers and even the neighbor's dog, swears by their iPhones. And what's fascinating is how they all seem to have this relentless mission to convert me. But here's the kicker: not one of them has ever given me a compelling reason why. The common thread? They simply believe the iPhone is superior – the ultimate pinnacle of technology. And you know what? That mindset didn't just materialize out of thin air; it was meticulously crafted over years of marketing tactics and societal pressures.

Now, when we shift gears to the fitness realm, it's a similar story. You dip your toes into the fitness world, start seeing some gains, maybe get a few compliments here and there. Next thing you know, you're doling out advice to friends, training buddies at the gym, and suddenly a gym manager is offering you a job. It's a journey towards self-improvement that many embark on, but unfortunately, most never make it past the initial phase. They get caught in a cycle of starting and stopping, forever riding the fitness rollercoaster.

But here's the thing about successful salespeople: they see a brighter future for you and are determined to help you get there. Case in point: back when I was overseeing multiple gym locations in our metro area, I decided to do some recon at a rival gym. As I walked in, I was greeted by John, an employee who wasted no time getting to know me. Instead of bombarding me with sales pitches, he took a genuine interest in my fitness journey, asking about my goals and workout history.

But here's the kicker: as John was learning about me, I was learning about him too. And what I gathered was that he wasn't fully satisfied in his current role – he craved something more meaningful. So, I pitched him an opportunity, scrawling out a compensation plan on the back of his membership pricing sheet. And you know what? He took the bait and became one of our top salespeople.

Now, let's talk mindset. It's not just about positive self-talk or motivational podcasts – it's about envisioning the future you want for yourself and those around you. Sales isn't just about hitting targets; it's about building relationships, fostering trust, and rallying your team behind a shared vision. And sometimes, it means doing unconventional things – like pitching someone a job at their current gig.

Principle 2: Developing a Rockstar Team

Those who possess the ability to transform a toxic work environment into a thriving one are worth their weight in gold, impacting both the company's top and bottom lines.

I'll never forget the jarring words of a letter left on an empty desk at a gym in turmoil. It was clear the previous general manager had orchestrated a mass exodus, leaving me to pick up the pieces. With a staff shortage, malfunctioning systems, and a gym in dire need of a reboot, I faced a daunting challenge. I wrestled with tough decisions: Should I scramble to hire anyone willing to fill a role? Pull resources from other gyms to patch the gaps? Or throw in the towel and pass the problem along? Amidst the chaos, I had to remind myself of one thing: I knew what I was looking for, and I knew how to build a stellar team.

So, I rolled up my sleeves and got to work. While I leaned on employees from other locations to keep things afloat, I was meticulous in my hiring process. I conducted nearly 40 interviews, passing on candidates with impressive resumes in favor of those who embodied hunger, humility, and a willingness to learn. This gym needed more than just experienced individuals; it needed people who were willing to roll up their sleeves and figure things out alongside me.

Once I had a solid management team in place, we turned our attention to the community. We hired trainers from among our long-time members, investing in their certification. We recruited individuals from various backgrounds who exemplified our company's values, taking the time to understand their personal goals and motivations. We didn't just throw them into roles; we treated them like valued members of our team, celebrating milestones and fostering a sense of camaraderie.

This approach paid dividends. Not only did it foster an exceptional team culture, but it also propelled the club to consistently meet and exceed its goals. Building a rockstar team isn't about finding unicorns with perfect experience; it's about hiring based on shared values and investing in each individual's growth. By demonstrating genuine care and interest in our team members, we cultivated loyalty and dedication. And while people may come and go, the ability to connect and empower others is a leadership skill that lasts a lifetime.

Principle 3: Developing Goals

Not too long ago, I found myself jetting off to Austin, Texas every month to lead franchisee inductions for a fitness brand. It was an eye-opening experience, meeting a diverse array of franchise owners – from eager newcomers to seasoned industry veterans. What struck me most was not just what these owners had in mind for their goals, but what they didn't have: clear expectations.

Questions about setting monthly targets, opening member counts, and operating expenses often drew blank stares. And that's when I realized the importance of starting with the end in mind. Instead of spoon-feeding answers, I'd flip the question back to them: What did they truly want to achieve? How much profit were they aiming for? Did they envision growth or were they content with steady income?

Some might see this approach as evasive, but even Jesus himself, in the Bible, responded to questions with questions. He understood that people often seek easy answers instead of grappling with deeper truths. And in business, we face the same dilemma – we must define our ultimate objectives and work backward from there.

This approach clarifies whether modest growth aligns with our financial goals or if we need to scale up to achieve our desired outcomes. And while it might seem daunting, the beauty of the fitness industry lies in its simplicity. There are essentially four avenues for business growth:

1. **Marketing Goals:** Understand your ideal customers to attract similar leads.
2. **Member Monthly Revenue Goals:** Increase purchases or upsell higher-value memberships.
3. **Retention Goals:** Foster a sense of community and accountability to keep members engaged.

4. **Sales Goals:** Manage member churn and conversion rates for sustained growth.

As you embark on goal-setting, remember the importance of mindset and collaboration. Clearly explain why goals are set as they are and invite input from your team. This not only fosters a sense of ownership but also cultivates a culture of continuous improvement. When your team grows, so does your business.

Principle 4: Accountability

"If anyone builds on this foundation using gold, silver, costly stones, wood, hay or straw, their work will be shown for what it is, because the Day will bring it to light. It will be revealed with fire, and the fire will test the quality of each person's work. If what has been built survives, the builder will receive a reward. If it is burned up, the builder will suffer loss but yet will be saved—even though only as one escaping through the flames." 1 Corinthians 3:12-15

It's widely acknowledged that in the realm of fitness business, quality reigns supreme over quantity. This principle extends beyond client accountability and class attendance to encompass the quality of every interaction, including outbound calls to prospects.

Not too long ago, I found myself taking on the daunting task of reviving multiple failing gyms in the Midwest. The company I worked for had expanded too rapidly, leaving a trail of operational chaos in its wake. My mission was clear: turn these gyms around.

During my first week at one of the gyms, I observed the assistant manager clicking through calls on the CRM system – calls that, as it turned out, he wasn't actually making. Instead of reprimanding him outright, I decided to engage in some role play. Despite his boasts about sales prowess, our interaction revealed his shaky grasp of the fundamentals. It dawned on me that his apparent success was more a result of receiving high-quality digital leads rather than his own sales acumen.

I made a commitment to him: I would support his personal and career goals if he committed to daily role-playing sessions with me. While his call and appointment numbers initially dropped, I wasn't fazed. These were now genuine interactions, leading to real appointments and meaningful connections with potential clients.

My approach to holding him accountable went beyond mere metrics – I focused on the effectiveness of his role. When setting accountability standards for your team, it's essential to look beyond the numbers and understand the underlying story. Low show rates, poor class attendance, or high turnover may signal deeper issues that require attention.

Regular check-ins are invaluable for understanding your business, but true accountability flows both ways. As a leader, you must be attuned to the daily realities of your team. How can you effectively manage if you're not intimately familiar with the day-to-day operations?

In a world inundated with purported solutions, it's easy to get lost in a sea of contradictory advice. Allow me to share a personal anecdote: While traveling for a presentation, I found myself booked at a different hotel from the venue. My Uber driver's playful jab – "They don't even make room for you here? You must not be very good!" – served as a humorous reminder that humility is key. It's not about me; it's about serving others.

This principle holds true in the fitness industry, where every sale represents an opportunity to transform lives. Whether it's empowering an elderly woman to live independently or helping a struggling single mom find stability, the impact of our work transcends mere financial gains. It's about making a lasting difference in the lives of real people, one sale at a time.

💡 Actionable Tips

In the pursuit of cultivating a robust sales culture within your business, it's crucial to equip yourself and your team with actionable strategies that drive success. This section offers a comprehensive guide to implementing key practices that foster growth and effectiveness. From embracing a growth mindset to prioritizing cultural fit during hiring, defining specific goals, conducting regular performance reviews, and providing ample support for professional development, these tips provide a roadmap for building a sales-centric environment that thrives on continuous improvement and achievement. By incorporating these principles into your business, you can elevate performance, drive results, and nurture a sales culture that propels your organization forward.

1. **Embrace a Growth Mindset:** Cultivate a growth mindset that embraces challenges and sees failure as an opportunity for learning and growth. Instead of being deterred by setbacks, view them as valuable lessons that help you improve and refine your approach. Stay open-minded, adaptable, and willing to step outside your comfort zone to achieve your goals.
2. **Prioritize Cultural Fit:** During the hiring process, prioritize cultural fit over technical skills or experience. Look for candidates who not only possess the necessary qualifications but also resonate with your company's values and mission. Conduct behavioral interviews, ask situational questions, and seek examples of how candidates have demonstrated your core values in their previous roles.
3. **Define Specific, Measurable Goals:** Start by clearly defining your business goals in specific and measurable terms. Instead of vague

aspirations like "increase revenue," set specific targets such as "achieve a 10% increase in monthly revenue" or "reduce member churn rate by 15%." This clarity will provide a clear direction for your efforts and enable you to track progress effectively.

4. **Implement Regular Performance Reviews and Feedback Sessions:** Schedule regular one-on-one meetings with team members to review their performance, provide constructive feedback, and address any concerns or challenges they may be facing. Use these sessions as opportunities to celebrate successes, identify areas for improvement, and set action plans for achieving goals. By providing consistent feedback and support, you can help your team members stay on track and continuously improve.

5. **Provide Support and Resources for Growth:** Invest in the professional development and growth of your team members by providing them with the necessary support, resources, and opportunities for learning and skill development. Offer training programs, coaching sessions, and mentorship opportunities to help them enhance their knowledge, skills, and capabilities. By investing in your team's growth, you not only empower them to perform at their best but also demonstrate your commitment to their success and development.

Connect

If you're a fitness business owner grappling with the challenge of consistently meeting your targets, seeking clarity on which metrics to focus on, and eager to achieve your long-held goals, partnering with a mentor and coach could be the solution you need. Ben offers freelance consulting services, fractional executive work in operations, sales, marketing, hiring, staff development, and culture building. He's also open to exploring partnership opportunities.

To determine if a partnership with Ben is the right fit for you, reach out to him for an introductory meeting. You can contact him directly at bcludwig8338@gmail.com and find him on LinkedIn at linkedin.com/in/ben-ludwig-a57ab169, where he frequently shares insightful articles and features on effectively managing fitness businesses.

ABOUT THE AUTHOR

Ben Ludwig is an accomplished leadership, sales, and strategy expert with extensive experience in the fitness industry. As a fractional executive, he specializes in working with fitness startups and global brands, offering invaluable insights and guidance. With a proven track record, Ben has partnered with numerous fitness brands, providing leadership and strategic direction.

Ben's expertise extends to global training initiatives, where he has conducted sessions on fitness sales, marketing, and operations across more than 60 countries. He is a sought-after speaker, delivering engaging seminars both in-person and virtually for fitness business owners worldwide. Additionally, Ben has developed impactful sales materials for owners and brands on a global scale.

Currently serving as the Chief Operating Officer of Traction Group LLC, an F45 Training company, Ben brings his wealth of experience to drive growth and success. He also holds the role of Growth Pastor for CrosspointNow Network of Churches across Kansas, reflecting his commitment to community and service.

Beyond his professional roles, Ben is a prolific contributor to various fitness business magazines, including Fitness Business Insider Magazine, Club Solutions, Club Industry, PFP Magazine, and Gym Owner Monthly. He generously volunteers his time on multiple boards, leveraging his expertise to support causes aligned with his values.

Ben's dedication to excellence and his passion for making a difference make him a valuable asset to any organization or cause fortunate enough to benefit from his expertise.

CHAPTER 8
Do the Thing that Scares You:
The Vital Link Between Personal Fulfillment and Business Success

by Rachele Evers

📝 The Story

Let's kick off by addressing the essence of this narrative. Undoubtedly, the pivotal choice that has propelled both my business achievements and, fundamentally, my personal fulfillment, was liberating myself from the influence of others' opinions on my decisions.

Stop believing what other people tell you you need to do. This includes me, and any takeaways you may get from reading my story. I know that sounds counterintuitive, but it's true. Don't let me, or anyone, tell you what to do with your life. Having said that, here is how I went from being an angry, frustrated, unfulfilled, overworked, lost and sad woman to the powerful, satisfied, successful, happy and fulfilled person I am today.

Preface/Setting

Imagine a woman, say 40 or so years old, divorced with 3 children ages 12, 13, & 14. This woman has a decent enough corporate job that pays just fine, but it's barely enough to stay afloat, and she's just left her second marriage which, unlike the first one, has cost her literally everything. This woman has only enough money to pay rent on the house she needs for her and her kids to live in. For the past 6 years she's been working 3 jobs just to stay above water. Her main job is in Corporate America, with bartending on the side, and sporadic retail sales positions just to make ends meet. She hasn't seen her kids much because she's the only breadwinner and someone has to pay the bills.

This woman is exhausted, running on adrenaline and caffeine. Waking up early to get kids on their buses, driving to aforementioned corporate job, working all day, then leaving in the evening to go do a shift at the bar. Often running to the grocery store after closing the bar, ultimately arriving home long after everyone else is in bed. Go to sleep. Wake up. Do it all again.

This is Exhausting. Soul-crushing. This lifestyle is literally killing her.

But what else is there to do?

That woman was me 10 years ago.

Let's back up a bit.

My senior year of undergrad I married my high school sweetheart at age 21. Fresh out of college, we immediately started our family and had 3 beautiful children. After a dozen or so years of marriage, it became clear to both of us that this was not what either of us wanted.

I wasn't sure why I didn't want that life. I had done everything by the book to have a happy life. Literally *everything*.

Good grades? Check.

College Degree? Check.

Married? Check.

New House? Check.

New Car? Check.

Requisite number of kids? Check.

I had checked all the boxes dammit! And right around 30 years old I looked around and realized that my entire life was based on things that other people had told me to want. The boxes were checked, but I was miserable. It didn't make any sense. I was supposed to have made it! Everyone in my life thought I had it made, had the best life! My life looked good on paper, even to me, but I was empty inside. I couldn't figure out how to make my theoretically perfect life feel fulfilling. I just didn't love it. I had all of the pieces in place that you're supposed to have, so why did it feel so pointless? Why did I feel so worn out all the time? Where was the magic that is supposed to come with doing things right? My first marriage was perfectly fine and perfectly boring. Even though it was hard and sad, my first husband and I amicably divorced.

Here the story gets even better, because I married another man almost immediately and *I made the same mistake, again, at a much larger scale.*

I thought that by changing my outside circumstances, I would be able to change my inside circumstances — how I felt about my life. I fully expected this new arrangement to be better than the old one. More fulfilling, more exciting. I expected it to make my life complete and satisfied. I now had a new husband, his 3 kids, my 3 kids, and massive financial responsibilities. He didn't work. I worked more. He spent lots of money. I got lines of credit, and worked *even more*. I used the same strategies I had previously used to build my life, only in a new environment. I really could not figure out why I was still so angry, unfulfilled, empty, exhausted, and sad.

The reality of my life is that I was running around like a lunatic doing what I thought I was supposed to do to build a good life. I built it, I burned it to the ground, and then I *built the same thing again*, only with more responsibilities, dependents, and complexity.

Just to give you some additional context, as I stated earlier, my second marriage was to a man who had no job. He had no ambition but he had a massive drinking and drug abuse problem. He was a financial disaster with anger issues. In hindsight, I believe he married me because he thought I had money. With 3 kids of his own, I probably looked like a nice choice who would simultaneously raise his kids and take care of him. The joke was on him.

I was frazzled, exhausted, running around trying to keep all of the threads from unraveling, and in this second "new and improved" version of my life, my marriage had slowly turned into a sickeningly abusive rollercoaster.

It might be worth mentioning here how I went from one perfectly fine but unfulfilling marriage to a second marriage that was an emotional rollercoaster and a disaster. I had married my first husband out of a desire to fit in a box. I wanted to be married because that is what you were supposed to do. I married my second husband as a complete and total overcompensation for the first one. This second man was exciting. He was dynamic and charming and swept me off my feet. I am not kidding when I tell you that at the beginning of our relationship, he felt like the one. I was totally, completely, overwhelmingly intoxicated by his charm. He said all the right things to me. I felt like I could have the dream life I wanted with him. His huge personality seemed to fill the empty void I was living with. I believed I had discovered the person who would alleviate the emptiness gnawing within me. My knight in shining armor had arrived.

I was blind to every red flag. The tumultuous ride of emotions that was our relationship seemed exciting and fun at first. It diverted my attention from the underlying discontent that quietly permeated every aspect of my life.

After enduring six and a half chaotic years, striving to attain an elusive ideal of a "perfect life," I made a pivotal decision. With what little funds remained, I relocated with my children to a more affordable place, determined to turn things around. Keeping my steady job, I harbored a burning desire to finally achieve that elusive sense of success. Despite working tirelessly and sacrificing time with my children, at least I was free from the toxicity of my former spouse. It felt like a small victory amidst the storms.

Wrong.

Here I was — a 40 year old woman trying so hard to make it all work. I had been through the wringer and was strung out working 3 jobs, I was newly divorced (again!). To top it all off, I had no money and 3 kids to take care of. I was exhausted, scared, confused, and didn't know what to do except take the next step that was right in front of me at the time. I didn't have the bandwidth to think of anything long-term. What's for dinner this week? No clue. What's for dinner right now? Depends on what's in the fridge. That is the kind of timeframe I was operating with.

Constantly putting out fires.

Constantly reacting to situations.

Relentlessly getting back up and doing what needed to be done...because if not me, then who?

I had a respectable corporate job. I was a telecommunications sales agent for a well-known, national communications company. They paid me well — not super luxury lifestyle well — but well enough that everyone around me thought I had a "good job." This was the job I was raised to pursue! I grew up being taught that if I just got a 9-to-5 job with a good benefits package and regular hours, I'd have it made. I was a good girl and got a college degree just like I was supposed to, because that is what you had to do to *make it*. I had gotten good grades in high school and gotten some college scholarships which were definitely a requirement for *making it*. I had gotten married and started a family — all part of the *making it* package. One little blip when I divorced husband #1, but I had corrected that quickly by marrying #2.

Looking back at these pieces of my life, a pattern emerged. Recognizing that pattern and taking my power back is what stopped me from recreating yet another unfulfilling situation based on other people's rules. It is what has gotten me to where I am today and it is the foundation of this chapter.

So now here I was, newly divorced for a second time with two failed marriages under my belt. My corporate job sucked...*bad*. Every day I had to get up at a ridiculously inhuman hour to get myself ready, put my kids on the bus, commute 45 minutes to the office, work all day, commute 45 minutes home, get the kids, feed the kids, get everyone to bed, and start all over again the next day.

I am skipping a lot of the steps here, but anyone who runs a household knows this drill. It is so hard trying to keep it all together without losing your shit. And sometimes, running around like a crazy person actually keeps you occupied so much that you don't have the time or space to lose your shit. You just keep going, because that is all you have time to do.

I had removed the chaos of the second marriage, which was a massive relief, but now I was on my own. This was a terrifying responsibility. I was still trying to keep from sinking. I was still running on adrenaline. I was still striving to create a life that met the criteria of success. I didn't realize I was doing this, of course. I never stopped to question what I was actually trying to do with my life. I just knew it was hard. Impossibly hard.

And then one magical day, everything changed.

🎯 The Principle

I want to tell you that this was an epiphany day — that I had a stroke of luck that allowed me to clearly see what I needed to do to *truly* make it. I want to tell you that I miraculously managed to make the necessary changes that transformed my life into one of perfection. Alas, none of this could be farther from the truth.

What actually happened is that I broke. I snapped. *I just stopped scrambling.*

I could not keep all of the balls in the air. I could not keep all of the threads together. I could not keep playing the role of the woman who wanted the traditionally perfect relationship, house, car, kids, career, and retirement. All of the things that I was told I should have to live a fulfilling life.

I realized that I had built my entire life around wanting what other people told me to want, and I had made some massive mistakes trying to arrange it to suit that narrative.

The truth is:

I wanted freedom.
I wanted joy.
I wanted laughter and time with my kids.
I wanted to spend quality time with them instead of managing them.
I wanted to connect with people.
I wanted things that no one told me how to get.

So one day, I walked into work and quit my corporate job. I quit on the spot, and did not provide notice. *I did not quit like a good girl*. I quit like a woman who has had enough — like a woman who is teetering on the edge of her last nerve. I quit like a woman who is broken and scared and tired and simply no longer cares about what she is supposed to want or what she is supposed to do.

When I quit my job, I had a dream in my back pocket. It was a dream I had wanted to chase but was too scared to try. It felt risky and it didn't fit the narrative of success that I had grown up with.

The previous year I had gotten my real estate license and thought I would add it to my ever-growing list of side gigs. I figured selling a couple of houses a month might help me with my financial situation. And here's the kicker: I had dreamed of being a real estate agent since I was a little girl, when my parents took me to their real estate agent's house for a meeting. The agent was the coolest, most glamorous woman I had ever seen! She was so pretty and nice and fancy. My little girl self was blown away by this woman and how she carried herself. I was enchanted by what it felt like to be in her presence. She had gotten in my psyche, and she got in deep.

I had gotten my real estate license and I had done nothing with it — until the day I had quit my job. It was *go* time.

In this new role, I didn't have anyone to report to. I had no boss, no clock, no pension, no benefits, no retirement. I also had no husband that I thought I had to report to. I only had myself, and I was now solely interested in being true and honest about the type of life *I* wanted to live. I was not going to chase someone else's dream or standards. I was not looking outside of myself to know what I wanted or to decide what I should do. It was terrifying! There was no corporation to tell me how to behave with a client, or what words to use in a given situation, or what product to push because it needed to be moved. There were no external boxes to check.

There was only me to answer to. It was completely new for me, and it was exhilarating. I was excited to find out what I could do!

I entered this new dream profession with fear and trepidation for sure, but also a new guiding force that I had never listened to before. I promised to be authentic, to be who I wanted to be in this role, and to want what *I* want out of life.

Through the act of quitting my corporate job, I opened up the possibility of chasing my own dreams. I stopped paying attention to what other people said I should want, and started exploring what I really wanted for my life. I was not putting my definition of happiness outside of myself. I was not following the rules (as I understood them). In my life up until this point, I had been driven to create a life that someone else defined for me.

My first marriage matched a fairytale notion of marrying my high school sweetheart and checking all of the boxes for a white picket fence life. I never stopped to wonder if I wanted something else.

My second marriage matched a story about finding my true love, and that would fix everything. The childhood knight-in-shining armor fairytale had me believing that the love of my life would somehow make my life perfect. I was so sure this was the key that I never stopped to wonder if I wanted something else.

My entire work trajectory fit the bill for the career that I was told to have. A career with a pension and 401(k) plan. Give 40 years to "the man", then enjoy your retirement.

Here is the golden nugget: I began my new career, my new life, with a specific drive to *no longer strive for a life I've been told to want.* This drive has steered every major decision I've made since.

So what does that look like? When I started my company, which was just me as an independent contractor at a local brokerage, I worked hard. All of those years with crushing responsibilities prepared me well for success in this highly competitive, sometimes cutthroat industry.

But instead of selling a product to meet a metric, this time I was helping people. I was obsessed with the idea that people need someone to advocate for them, look out for them where they can't, and walk with them through what is arguably the largest most emotional financial transaction of their lives.

I made it my business to learn everything about my industry. I became an expert at contracts and contract language. I became fluent in all the ways that real estate agents serve and advocate for their clients. I refined myself and my skills to ensure that I was always doing the best job possible for the people who hired me.

I could go on and on about the logistical things that I did...the classes, the certifications, the continuing education, the networking, and blah blah blah. But what really matters is this: I was driven by doing right by others. I was no longer trying to *make it*. It was magical. It still is magical.

By letting go of what others told me to want, I have given myself the freedom to define my life on my own terms. Because of this, I am able to serve my industry and my clients from the best possible perspective. Everything I do is built to serve the best interests of my clients *above all else*. Rather than just selling the widget out of necessity (as often happens in corporate jobs), I actively assist my clients in identifying their best interests and then support them accordingly.

- I ensure my clients are fully informed to make educated decisions and support them throughout the process.
- Clients are made aware of their obligations, potential exposure, and the necessary steps for achieving success.
- Decisions prioritize the client's best interests above all else.
- Our processes, contracts, mission statement, and vision are tailored to support our team in serving our clients' best interests.

- We leverage professional relationships to enhance our client service.
- Every step is evaluated to ensure it aligns with serving our clients' best interests.

Once I started operating from an inside perspective to define what I want in my life and support others in achieving their goals, instead of constantly seeking external validation, I gained clarity on the path to fulfillment.

I have grown from a single agent company to a broker/owner and partner of 3 real estate brokerages. I own some real estate investments, am an active member of my community, have served on multiple non-profit boards, host yoga at my office, and offer energy services in addition to real estate services. I travel often and have dinner with my kids at least once a week. I have beautiful relationships with my ex step children and with their mothers. I have a great relationship with my first ex-husband and his partner. I have a wonderful man in my life. Despite all the challenges I faced to get here, the most remarkable realization is that I became acutely aware that nothing enters my life without my consent.

Everything I desire in life stems from my aspiration to assist others in achieving their own goals. I've shifted away from seeking external validation to define my desires or determine the path to happiness.

I don't know how to wrap this up without it sounding like a trope or some kind of life lesson, which is not my intent at all. My hope is that someone out there (you) reading this story will be inspired to take the leap and do the thing that holds the key to the life *you* actually want to create for yourself. Not the life you were told to want. Not the life that looks good or matches what you see on TV. My hope is that you will be inspired to take the action that scares you before you get to your breaking point.

Do the thing that scares you. Make the move toward the life you want.

💡 Actionable Tips

In the journey towards personal fulfillment and professional success, the power of self-definition and authentic purpose cannot be overstated. Drawing from my own experiences, here are actionable tips to guide you towards self-discovery, growth, and the pursuit of your true aspirations.

1. **Define Your Own Path:** Take the time to reflect inwardly and identify what truly brings you fulfillment and purpose in life. Rather than seeking validation from external sources, trust your instincts and define your own goals and aspirations.
2. **Embrace Growth and Expansion:** Don't limit yourself to conventional boundaries. Allow yourself to grow and expand beyond your initial expectations. Take calculated risks and pursue opportunities for personal and professional development, even if they seem daunting at first.
3. **Serve Others Authentically:** Shift your focus from seeking validation to genuinely assisting others in achieving their goals. By prioritizing the needs and well-being of others, you create meaningful connections and contribute positively to your community and professional endeavors.
4. **Courageously Pursue Your Dreams:** Don't wait for a breaking point to take action. Embrace courage and take the leap toward the life you desire, even if it means stepping outside of your comfort zone. Trust that by facing your fears and pursuing your dreams, you'll uncover new opportunities for growth and fulfillment.

Connect

If you'd like to have a peek at my new and awesome authentic life that is full of jokes, laughter, references, music and real estate — or if you just want to chat or swap stories, find me here:

www.facebook.com/RacheleEversRealtor
www.instagram.com/therachelechristine/
linktr.ee/racheleevers

ABOUT THE AUTHOR

Meet Rachele Evers, a dynamic force of nature blending the worlds of real estate prowess and spiritual enlightenment. At 49 years old, Rachele navigates the bustling worlds of business ownership, agent inspiration, & property transactions while nurturing the soulful journey of her clients and community. With a career that started at 9 years old with a paper route, Rachele earned her stripes as a business woman and is a top-producing agent, consistently exceeding expectations and setting new standards of excellence. Her eye for detail, unwavering dedication, and innate ability to connect with clients on a profound level have cemented her reputation as a trusted advisor and confidante in the competitive real estate industry.

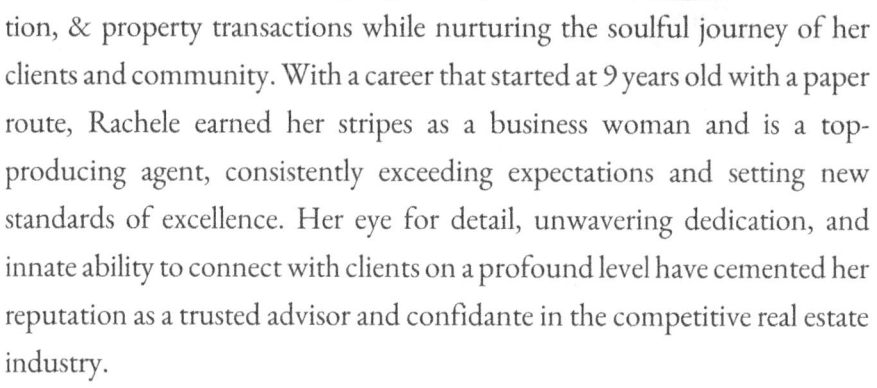

Beyond the boardrooms and open houses, she is a beacon of light in spiritual wellness, serving as a certified energy worker, yoga instructor, and Reiki master. Guided by her passion for holistic healing and personal growth, Rachele seamlessly weaves together the principles of mindfulness, compassion, and energetic alignment to empower her clients to embrace a life of balance, abundance, and fulfillment. Rachele approaches each endeavor with a rare blend of professionalism, warmth, and authenticity. Her infectious energy, unwavering optimism, and genuine love for what she does shine through in every interaction, leaving a lasting impression on all who cross her path.

CHAPTER 9

Lessons of Resilience

Navigating Adversity on the Path to Success

by Adolfo Ayala

The Story

In 2006, I found myself at a pivotal moment in my life. Despite a successful career at a Fortune 500 company, I couldn't shake the feeling that there was more to life than what I was experiencing. It was during a flight back to Los Angeles that I made the life-altering decision to resign from my job of eight years. The realization dawned on me that I was yearning for something beyond the confines of corporate life. With only a handful of sporadic service calls from dental offices to my name, I took a leap of faith into the unknown world of entrepreneurship.

The decision to embark on this journey was met with a mixture of disappointment and optimism from friends and family. The weight of responsibility felt heavier with a young family to support – an 11-year-old daughter and a 4-year-old son. The thought of risking stability for the uncertainty of entrepreneurship was daunting, but deep down, I held onto the belief that I could always return to the corporate world if things didn't work out.

As I ventured into the realm of entrepreneurship, I faced challenges and uncertainties that I had never encountered before. Yet, there was a sense of excitement and possibility in forging my own path. Each day brought new lessons and experiences, shaping me into a more resilient and determined individual. While the road ahead was uncertain, I was fueled by the belief that taking risks and pursuing my passions would ultimately lead to fulfillment and success.

As I reflect on the first year of my entrepreneurial journey, it's clear that it was a period of both challenges and unexpected opportunities. Having a severance package provided some financial cushioning, but navigating the landscape of creating and running my own business was far from intuitive. Unlike some individuals for whom entrepreneurship comes naturally, I found myself grappling with uncertainties about how to approach various aspects, from setting prices to marketing strategies. Recognizing the value of seeking guidance from those with more experience, I reached out to executives for advice, despite my initial discomfort with seeking help.

As the second year unfolded, it marked a turning point in my entrepreneurial endeavors. It seemed as though I had finally begun to gain traction and find my footing in the business world. The economy was thriving, and my business started to experience unprecedented growth. However, the promising outlook was abruptly disrupted by the onset of the 2008 financial crisis. The collapse of the housing market led to the voiding of many contracts, leaving me at a crossroads. Faced with uncertainty, I made the decision to pivot and explore alternative avenues to sustain my business.

One such opportunity arose in the form of warranty repair services. While initially seen as a temporary solution to weather the economic downturn, it unexpectedly opened doors to a new realm of possibilities.

Through interactions with clients in their homes, I identified a growing need for IT services, particularly in the context of home automation and audio-visual installations. Recognizing the pivotal role of network infrastructure in these setups, I began offering specialized IT services tailored to the needs of the audio-visual industry. This strategic shift not only diversified my business offerings but also positioned me at the forefront of a burgeoning market niche.

The success in expanding my business was fueled by the robust database of customers we had cultivated through our warranty repair services. Leveraging these existing relationships, I proactively engaged with clients to address their evolving audio-visual (AV) and IT system needs. By offering tailored solutions and exceptional service, we solidified our position as trusted partners in the industry.

However, the subsequent years presented formidable challenges as I navigated the nuances of transitioning from commercial to home service operations. The demands and expectations of homeowners proved to be vastly different, often requiring round-the-clock availability and personalized attention. Recognizing the need for specialized expertise in operational management, I made the strategic decision to seek a business partner who could complement my skill set.

Enter my business partner, whose decision to join forces marked a pivotal moment in our entrepreneurial journey. Together, we embarked on a shared mission to elevate our business to new heights. Despite facing setbacks and obstacles along the way, our unwavering resilience, hope, and faith served as guiding beacons through turbulent times.

Drawing strength from my upbringing and spiritual beliefs, I embraced the notion that challenges were not insurmountable roadblocks but rather opportunities for growth and learning. With a steadfast resolve and unwavering faith in a higher purpose, I confronted adversity head-on, confident that every obstacle was a stepping stone towards greater success. Through perseverance and an indomitable spirit, I fortified myself with the courage and resilience needed to navigate life's unpredictable journey.

I've come to realize that amidst life's storms, there's often an opportunity for growth and transformation. Embracing change and adapting to evolving circumstances have become essential skills in navigating the unpredictable journey of entrepreneurship. Reflecting on pivotal moments like the one in 2008, I recognize that my decision to pivot was instrumental in shaping the trajectory of my business. Had I not embraced change during that tumultuous period, I can only speculate on the missed opportunities and unexplored potentials that would have ensued.

Fast forward to the present day, and the ethos of adaptation and resilience remains at the core of our business philosophy. We understand the value of continual learning and the power of collaboration in overcoming challenges. The lessons gleaned from the trials of 2008 were not only profound but also instrumental in forging valuable partnerships, like the one with my exemplary business partner.

As a result of our collective efforts and unwavering commitment to growth, Active Networks LLC has undergone a remarkable transformation. While our initial focus may have been primarily commercial, our clientele has evolved organically over the years, with residential clients constituting the majority of our business. This unforeseen shift underscores the dynamic nature of entrepreneurship and the importance of remaining adaptable to changing market dynamics.

Actionable Tips

Hope, faith, and resilience are essential tools for navigating the journey of life and entrepreneurship. Within each individual lies untapped potential and greatness waiting to be unleashed. By cultivating a mindset of hope and maintaining unwavering faith in one's abilities, you can confront challenges with resilience and determination, propelling yourself towards success in the long run.

Our daily choices are pivotal in shaping our paths and determining our outcomes. Emotions and self-perception have a profound influence in our decision-making processes, urging us to introspect and assess our responses to various situations. By posing reflective questions such as "What type of person am I?" and "What would a person like me do in this situation?" we can gain valuable insights into our values, beliefs, and behavioral tendencies. This intentional self-awareness enables us to make informed decisions aligned with our authentic selves, ultimately guiding us towards our desired goals.

Lastly, I hope that my chapter leads you to a practice of intentional mindfulness and active listening in your decision-making processes. I cannot express how important it is to pause amidst the hustle and bustle of daily life to listen to your inner voice and external cues. By being present in the moment and attuned to the nuances of your surroundings, you can discern valuable insights and intuitive guidance that may inform your choices. This is a deliberate approach to decision-making that can empower you to navigate challenges with clarity and purpose, which will facilitate your journey towards personal and professional fulfillment.

🔗 Connect

Ready to dive deeper into stories of resilience, growth, and entrepreneurship? Connect with me on Instagram and Facebook @therealadolfo! Let's embark on this journey together, sharing insights, inspiration, and support along the way. Don't miss out on exclusive content and updates. See you there!

ABOUT THE AUTHOR

I'm Adolfo Ayala, and my story isn't just about success—it's about resilience. I believe in remaining a perpetual student in the ever-evolving game of life. With each experience, I uncover valuable lessons and insights. I'm passionate about supporting individuals and groups who, like me, are pursuing authentic dreams. Let's journey together towards realizing our true potential.

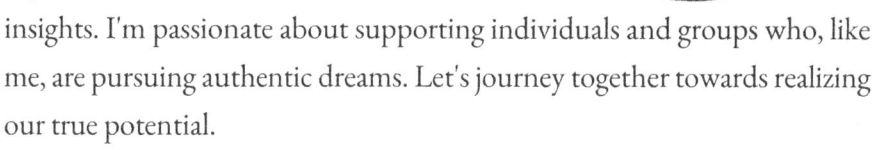

CHAPTER 10

Creativity Sus 'Pen' ded:

The Role of Creativity in Business Differentiation and Success

by Skylar Sullivan

> *"There is nothing to writing. All one must do is sit with a favorite pen in hand and bleed."*
> - Earnest Hemingway

The Story

Hello and welcome to my shop.

I firmly believe that your business, your entrepreneurship – the means by which you provide for yourself and your family – is the purest form of creativity known to humanity. Sales copy, marketing advertisements, your core values, and life's truths are all expressions of yourself, distilled to their essence. Even the most basic sales copy is simply part of the art you're creating.

Yes, I understand, we draw inspiration from our consumers, our ideal clients, but ultimately, it originates from within us. Consider a technical document. Its significance stems from the person who authored it, who pondered over what steps are crucial and worth sharing.

As we reflect on our past, with all its stories, knowledge, and life experiences, we utilize it to forge ahead, to create more and strive for improvement in every facet of life. Creativity isn't just a word or a simple action; it's what enables us to be most authentic.

When making purchasing decisions, we don't choose based on minor details like the placement of a pixel in marketing material. Instead, we buy from those we trust and know. What defines trust and familiarity?

Interaction and authenticity are crucial aspects of engagement.

Interaction may seem straightforward—it includes activities like posting, commenting on social media, active participation in the community, and addressing questions. It's about being present and engaged.

Authenticity, on the other hand, is more nuanced, requiring a touch of creativity. While you can stick to the basics and follow conventional methods, true authenticity involves creativity. In marketing, all strategies have the potential to work, but being creative sets you apart. It's akin to adding a motor to your bike, enhancing your speed.

The simplest way to infuse creativity and authenticity into your endeavors is by incorporating personal stories into your work—something meaningful to you. This is where the journey truly begins.

That's the first step to being more creative: incorporate personal stories into your work.

As a child, I was captivated by geology—crystals, gemstones, minerals, fossils, and yes, even rocks. There's something mesmerizing about the swirls of color trapped in a geode, evoking a sense of joy and warmth reminiscent of childhood memories.

Even today, I'm still enamored with those colorful swirls and the simplicity found in geodes. As an artisan carpenter, I aimed to capture that same passion and wonder in a handmade, one-of-a-kind pen. For me, the immediate sale of such a pen isn't the priority; it's about creating something that resonates deeply with someone, sparking that undeniable feeling of "I need THAT pen."

I'm a naturally curious individual, finding fascination in small tidbits of knowledge. While I blend various facets of creativity, I thoroughly enjoy the process of research and learning, often incorporating fun facts into my work. After all, who doesn't love a good trivia tidbit? For instance, did you know that the opposite sides of a standard six-sided dice always add up to seven? It's these little discoveries that fuel my creativity.

Creativity is vital because it breathes life into our existence, infusing it with purpose and joy. Despite having stable metrics and measurable success, we can often find ourselves suffocating under the weight of monotony, like being trapped under a heavy blanket. It's comfortable yet stifling, draining us of our energy and enthusiasm.

I've experienced this first hand earlier in my career when doubts about my skills and purpose crept in, casting a shadow of uncertainty over my work. I questioned whether people genuinely appreciated what I did, or worse, if I secretly despised it myself. These doubts grew, tightening their grip on my chest until I felt suffocated by uncertainty.

During a walk through a local park, something I rarely did, I stumbled upon limestone cuts along the path. What seemed mundane at first revealed itself to be a treasure trove of fossils—shell imprints, sponge balls, and even fish skeletons. Despite being made of the same elements and composition, each limestone cut was uniquely different, inviting me to see things from a new perspective. It was a moment of clarity, a metaphorical lightbulb illuminating my path forward.

That's the second step to being more creative: do something different.

It doesn't have to be a drastic change or a whole new career path; sometimes, it's just about doing something a bit different. For me, it was stepping outside my comfort zone, but for many others, it could be as simple as reading a book, catching up with an old friend, or jotting down thoughts in a journal.

As I rushed home from the greenway, my mind was buzzing with ideas for creating a geode pen—a concept I'd been mulling over in my idea journal for years. It felt like a leap into uncharted territory, but I didn't let that stop me. Even if this pen ended up being just for me, its uniqueness excited me. I remembered how Stanley introduced a pink cup for variety, sparking a frenzy on the internet. So what if my pen wasn't perfect? It would still stand out, just like Stanley's pink cup.

Amidst my brainstorming, doubts crept in. What if nobody liked it? I reminded myself that it didn't matter; what mattered was pursuing something I found exciting. Sure, making these pens might be costly and time-consuming, and there was a risk of failure. But I decided to push aside those doubts and take a chance.

On a whim, I posted a simple question on Facebook, putting my idea out into the world.

"I have this really neat idea for a pen based on a geode, but I'm stuck on colors. What do you think?"

Initially, there was silence, but then a friend reached out—a sign that perhaps my idea wasn't as crazy as I thought.

That's the third step to being more creative: your existing customers, followers, and associates are your greatest sounding board.

I prefer a close-knit circle of trustworthy individuals who don't sugarcoat things. While face-to-face gatherings are usually best, social media has its own unique charm, especially when you're miles apart from everyone else.

As it turned out, her cousin was finally graduating college with a PhD in volcanology after a long journey. Volcanology, often joked about as the study of Vulcans like from Star Trek, is actually the study of earth movements, volcanoes, and the earth itself—a kind of advanced geology. Through our conversation, I learned a bit about her cousin: he attended the University of Texas, was deeply passionate about his field, and had a fondness for the color blue. Suddenly, the vague concept I had for the pen sprang to life in my mind.

Interrupting her mid-sentence, I confidently exclaimed, "I've got this." With her approval, I described my vision for the pen: a silver and gold-trimmed body made of sturdy cherry wood, showcasing pronounced layers near the sap line. Tiny hand-cast resin crystals would adorn the pen, set against a slightly less blue resin background, resembling a core sample from a geological expedition. She was immediately sold on the idea, but it was my creative vision that truly sold the pen.

Then came the meticulous process of selecting rock candy shapes to mimic quartz crystals—the main crystals found in geodes. Each piece of rock candy was cast in silicon, and the pen was meticulously crafted step by step. It was a fun but time-consuming process, with each color requiring an extra week to perfect.

Of course, there were setbacks along the way: the silicon absorbing the candy, the resin curing too quickly and becoming brittle, the pen shattering, and the layers failing to bond. Yet, throughout the journey, I felt a sense of joy and wonder, relishing in the exploration of something new and the satisfaction of overcoming challenges. I diligently documented each failure, noting casting techniques and resin types, all while embracing the writing process itself.

Just for the record, that pen? *It's awesome.*

But let's rewind a bit. This pen would've never come to be if I hadn't acknowledged my deep-rooted love for geology. Once it was complete and ready to send off, I took a moment to document each step meticulously—a sort of personal record. Alongside this, I penned a letter to my customer and another to the intended recipient.

Now, why all this emphasis on handwriting? Well, it's a crucial step in the creative process—both the first and the last, you might say. Simply sitting down and putting ink to paper is where it all begins and ends.

Consider this: when was the last time you received a handwritten letter? For most of my clients, it's the handwritten note I include with each order. Sure, it takes a bit longer to ship, but there's a depth of emotion and personality in each stroke of my handwriting that's simply not present in a typed letter—no matter how fancy the font.

Handwriting is, in many ways, a lost art form. But imagine the impact it can have—mistakes and all—compared to a typed note. It shows the recipient that you've taken the extra time to acknowledge them, and that's something people respect—whether they're clients, family, or friends.

Moreover, there's science behind it: writing stimulates the same neurons in our brains as learning does, making us far more likely to remember what we've written—up to 75% more likely, in fact. And if we use a special pen? That boosts the retention rate to nearly 95%. Why? Because writing, in essence, is an art form—a tool for creativity!

Now, picture this: it's not just a thank-you letter; it's thank-you art. How much more impactful are those words now? It's not merely a few creative words on a page anymore.

Instead, it's paragraphs of heartfelt meaning—something both you, as the creator, and they, as the recipient, will remember. That, my friend, is truly something special.

🎯 The Principle

Reflecting on our past experiences, stories, and accumulated knowledge serves as a foundation for progress. It's from this reservoir of life's lessons that we draw inspiration to move forward, aiming for improvement in every aspect of our lives. Creativity, far from being a mere word or action, lies at the heart of authenticity, allowing us to express our true selves genuinely.

While interaction may seem straightforward, it's more than just engaging in social media activities or participating in community events. It's about active presence and genuine engagement. On the other hand, authenticity demands a touch of creativity. While conventional methods may suffice, true authenticity requires a creative twist. In the realm of marketing, where all strategies have potential, creativity acts as a turbo boost, setting you apart from the crowd.

Injecting personal stories into your work is the simplest yet most powerful way to infuse creativity and authenticity. By incorporating elements meaningful to you, whether it's a cherished memory or a deeply-held belief, you embark on a journey of true expression. This marks the second step towards unlocking your creative potential: embracing the power of uniqueness.

Creativity doesn't always require drastic changes or new career paths. Sometimes, it's as simple as doing something a little different. Whether it's stepping out of your comfort zone or exploring new interests, small deviations from the norm can spark creativity. Whether it's picking up a new hobby or reconnecting with old friends, every small step towards novelty contributes to your creative journey.

Finally, your existing network—customers, followers, and colleagues—serve as invaluable resources for feedback and inspiration. Engaging with them not only fosters deeper connections but also provides valuable insights into what resonates with your audience. They are the sounding board for your ideas, offering feedback and guidance as you navigate your creative endeavors. This marks the third step towards cultivating creativity: embracing the power of collaboration and feedback.

Actionable Tips

Unlocking your creative potential often involves a journey inward, drawing from your past experiences and personal stories. From reflecting on your past to engaging with your network, these strategies will empower you to tap into your unique voice and bring new depth to your endeavors.

1. Draw Inspiration from Your Past: Take time to reflect on your past experiences, stories, and knowledge. Identify key lessons and moments that have shaped you. Use these insights as a foundation for creative expression and personal growth in your endeavors.
2. Inject Personal Stories into Your Work: Incorporate elements of your own life into your projects, whether it's a cherished memory, a meaningful belief, or a unique experience. By infusing your work with personal stories, you add depth, authenticity, and relatability, connecting more deeply with your audience.

3. Engage with Your Network: Leverage your existing network of customers, followers, and colleagues as a valuable resource for feedback and inspiration. Actively engage with them, seek their input, and listen to their perspectives. Their insights can provide valuable guidance and help you refine your creative ideas and projects.

Connect

Ready to kickstart your journey to higher creativity and meaning? Visit theskymaker.com to explore our collection of unique, handmade pens that are as irreplaceable as they are inspiring. Whether you're looking for a ready-made gem or interested in a custom commission, I've got you covered. Plus, for an extra touch of fun, I'll even document the creation process in a personalized YouTube video for you to cherish and share. Let's make something unforgettable together!

ABOUT THE AUTHOR

Skylar Sullivan, born into a military family, embraced a life of constant movement, finding his roots not in a specific place, but in his passion and talent. Today, he wears multiple hats—as a creative consultant, the visionary owner of theskymaker, and a master furniture repair technician. With a singular focus on making the world more memorable and helping clients stand out in every detail, Skylar brings over 13 years of hands-on experience to his craft.

CHAPTER 11
Unlocking Potential and Empower Others:
The Lessons I Learned Alongside Bill

by Brent Knott

The Story

At 23 years old, I found myself at a crossroads. Frustrated with a less-than-stellar boss, I made the bold decision to leave my job. It was a move born out of necessity; I knew that sooner or later, someone cheaper or perhaps more skilled would replace me. So, armed with determination, I packed up everything I owned into my trusty 1991 Mazda Miata—a feat in itself, given the car's limited space. With a microwave doubling as extra storage for clothes, I hit the road with no clear plan but a fierce resolve to forge my own path.

In the midst of this uncertainty, a chance connection with a man named Pablo Zapata led me to Bill, who offered me an opportunity to sell a vehicle wrap for a Porsche Cayman. This was my lifeline—a chance to earn $6,000 and buy myself time to figure things out. There was even talk of a potential second Porsche, though nothing was certain. The catch? I had never wrapped a Porsche before, only my humble Miata and a Ford

F-150. Fear gnawed at me, but I've always been one to embrace the "get shit done" mentality.

With trembling hands, I drove down to Amelia Island, Florida, to meet the customer and secure the deposit. It was a nerve-wracking moment—I barely had enough money to cover the materials, let alone ask for a deposit. Imposter syndrome crept in; who was I to tackle such a prestigious project when I had only wrapped smaller vehicles before? Yet, with grit and determination, I pushed forward, seeing beyond the doubt to the opportunity that lay ahead.

With the deposit from Mr. Bill safely in hand, I made my way to a distributor in Jacksonville, where the chosen color resided in Hexus USA's warehouse. Not only was this my first time wrapping a car of such magnitude, but it was also my maiden voyage with this particular material. In the world of vehicle wraps, each film has its own quirks and intricacies during installation.

Fortune smiled upon me when I crossed paths with Jerry McConner while fetching water. Jerry, a seasoned veteran in the field, was coincidentally taking a break as well. It was a serendipitous encounter; Jerry, as I later discovered, had over 20 years of experience in installation and was highly respected in the industry.

Over a brief chat, Jerry imparted invaluable wisdom on handling Hexus materials, emphasizing the importance of adhering to the manufacturer's guidelines to the letter. His guidance was a lifeline, offering crucial insights into the nuances of the material and the meticulous finish work required for success.

Armed with Jerry's advice and the deposit, I procured the necessary materials and returned to the shop to tackle the Porsche. The process stretched over three weeks, longer than ideal, but the end result exceeded expectations. Despite a few minor imperfections, the finished product was a testament to my growing skill and dedication. The client's satisfaction spoke volumes, sealing the deal and affirming my journey into the world of vehicle wrapping.

My success with the first vehicle led to an opportunity to wrap a second car for Mr. Bill—a vintage Le Mans hippie style vehicle. However, unlike the first project, this one came with a unique challenge: the only reference provided was a miniature diecast model. Undeterred, I embarked on the task, resorting to manual methods like hand-cutting stripes using masking tape and manila folders. Without the luxury of computer-assisted design tools, every detail had to be meticulously crafted by hand. Despite the daunting nature of the task, I managed to streamline my installation time from three weeks to just ten business days.

Midway through the second project, Mr. Bill approached me with an unexpected inquiry about my future plans. Candidly, I admitted to being uncertain about my path forward, relying on the vehicle wraps as a means to sustain myself while I figured things out. His subsequent line of questioning, probing into my character and reactions, left me perplexed. It felt as though I was being scrutinized in ways beyond the scope of my job. However, his intentions became clearer when, at the project's conclusion, he challenged me to draft a business plan for a car wrapping venture.

Determined to rise to the occasion, I dedicated myself to researching and piecing together a comprehensive plan. Hours spent scouring YouTube for guidance culminated in a submission to Mr. Bill. Yet, his response was not what I expected. Instead of praise, he offered constructive criticism, likening my plan to "all buns and no meat." Undeterred, he pledged to mentor me upon his return from the races, signaling a pivotal moment in my journey towards entrepreneurship.

Under Mr. Bill's guidance, I delved deeper into crafting the business plan, pouring an additional 20 hours into the endeavor. Upon his return, his recognition of my work ethic bolstered my confidence, and he proceeded to offer invaluable insights on refining the plan. It was during this process that he broached the topic of equity split, a concept that initially left me flustered and uncertain. His straightforward question—what my contribution in sweat and time equated to in comparison to his financial investment—forced me to confront my own self-worth.

In a moment of naivety and realism, I proposed a lopsided split of 70-30 in his favor. It was a stark acknowledgment of the limitations of my current circumstances, coupled with a recognition of the potential gains for myself in our partnership. With a contract and business operations agreement in hand, our venture officially began.

Over the course of seven years, Bill proved to be an indispensable mentor, shaping me into the entrepreneur I am today. His business acumen, honed through the school of hard knocks, was unparalleled. Despite his gruff exterior and uncompromising demeanor, his dedication to my growth was unwavering. His love manifested in tough love—demanding accountability and excellence at every turn.

Our journey together was a roller coaster ride of highs and lows, but through it all, Bill's mentorship left an indelible mark on me. He challenged me, pushed me beyond my limits, and ultimately, set me on a path towards success. Looking back, I realize how fortunate I was to have him as a mentor, and I wish that everyone could experience the transformative power of such guidance.

By the third year of our partnership, the business began to gain traction, and profits started rolling in. Riding the wave of success, I found myself succumbing to the allure of my own accomplishments, allowing my ego to inflate. One particular incident stands out vividly in my memory—a heated debate with Bill over the purchase of a computer for our graphics department. I, being proficient in building computers, insisted on my way, declaring arrogantly, "Bill, I'm your business partner; you should listen to me." Reflecting on it now, I cringe at the audacity of my words and marvel at Bill's patience in tolerating such behavior.

By the fifth year, our fortunes continued to soar, with profits reaching unprecedented heights. However, despite our success, I found myself undervaluing my own contributions, continuing to perform installations without fair compensation. It was a pattern of self-deprecation that I failed to recognize until later.

During what should have been a celebratory moment of record-breaking profits, disaster struck in the form of an audit. Tasked with wrapping a significant project for a nonprofit organization, I found myself ill-prepared when Bill requested the project's spreadsheet for review. Ignorant of the personal connection between Bill and the organization, I offered only a rough estimate, prompting his fury.

In a moment of frustration, Bill delivered a sobering ultimatum, laying bare the consequences of my disregard for his guidance and the established operating procedures. His words cut deep, serving as a stark reminder of the responsibilities that came with our partnership. It was a wake-up call that forced me to confront my own shortcomings and the impact of my actions on our shared enterprise.

That pivotal moment marked a turning point in my relationship with Bill—I ceased making excuses and started taking responsibility for my actions. It's perplexing why it took me five years to reach this realization, but from that point on, I simply nodded and acknowledged his feedback during our meetings. Hard conversations became a regular occurrence, a testament to Bill's unwavering commitment to holding me accountable.

Despite the challenges, I remained in business with Bill not out of fear, but because deep down, I knew he was right. His business offered me an unparalleled opportunity, providing access to an unlimited credit line. In hindsight, my earlier confidence seemed misplaced, overshadowed by the reality of our partnership.

Fast forward to the seventh year—the year I finally mustered the courage to broach the topic of buying out Bill's stake in the business. Seeking guidance from individuals who had sold companies before, I explored various scenarios and ran the numbers to determine the cost of acquiring a 70% share based on our profitability. The estimates varied widely, with $100,000 - $225,000 as the median figure. Ultimately, I approached Bill with a proposal, prepared to negotiate terms.

To my astonishment, Bill's response was unexpected—he expressed a willingness to sell the business for a mere $25. Stunned by his generosity and relieved of the burden of securing a substantial sum, I realized the depth of his trust and faith in me. It was a humbling moment, a stark reminder of the value he placed on our partnership and the journey we had embarked on together.

Two to three years post-buyout, I found myself entrenched in the role of installer at the shop. Despite achieving financial success beyond anything I had experienced before, I remained committed to continuous self-improvement. I sought out a coach, a decision that raised eyebrows, including Bill's. His skepticism was palpable when he questioned why I was paying for guidance when I had received invaluable mentorship from him for seven years. Yet, my stubborn nature persisted, driving me to seek alternative paths to growth.

It wasn't until I joined my current mastermind group that I finally began to see a shift in the right direction. The collective wisdom and support of the group catalyzed a transformation within me, nudging me towards positive change.

Reflecting on my journey, I realized that Bill had been willing to sell the company to me as early as the third year—a fact I had failed to grasp at the time. His subtle hints about the potential life-changing opportunity went unnoticed, overshadowed by my own tunnel vision. Bill, always accommodating, granted me the exact terms I had requested, from ownership percentage to pay rate. It was a lesson in accountability—every decision and action I took had consequences, shaping the trajectory of my life and business.

Through Bill's tough love and the guidance of my mastermind peers, I learned the importance of taking decisive action and holding myself accountable. It was a transformative period marked by self-discovery and growth, one that ultimately propelled me towards a path of greater fulfillment and success.

Three or four years down the road, Bill remains a prominent figure in my life, evolving into a cherished father figure whom I affectionately refer to as my "business dad." With three shops under my belt, two of which operate under separate ownership agreements, our partnership continues to flourish. These agreements are structured to incentivize growth, with ownership or profit share increasing as revenue targets are met. For instance, at the outset, I hold an 80% ownership stake, while my partners hold the remaining 20%. However, as revenue milestones are achieved, their ownership share increases, reaching parity at certain revenue thresholds.

The impact of this arrangement is profound—it's not merely about profit but about catalyzing life-changing opportunities for my partners. Crossing the million-dollar revenue mark signifies a monumental shift in their lives, a testament to the transformative power of entrepreneurship. My role has evolved into that of a coach and mentor, guiding them through the intricacies of business ownership and empowering them to seize these opportunities.

In essence, my journey has taken on a new purpose—I'm not just building my own companies; I'm uplifting others along the way. Inspired by Bill's mentorship, I've made it my life's mission to create opportunities for those around me, believing that by helping others achieve their dreams, I'll inevitably realize my own.

As I reflect on my journey, I am filled with gratitude towards Bill. He was the catalyst for change, the architect of my transformation, and for that, I owe him a debt of gratitude. His belief in me paved the way for countless opportunities, and it's my sincerest hope that I can pay it forward, inspiring others to reach for the stars and touch the lives of those around them.

🎯 The Principle

Resilience and Adaptability: At 23, I found myself facing a daunting decision—to leave my job due to a difficult boss. With determination coursing through my veins, I packed all my possessions into a 1991 Mazda Miata and set out on an uncertain journey. Despite the uncertainty looming ahead, I embraced the challenges, showcasing resilience and adaptability as I navigated the unknown.

Embrace of Mentorship and Continuous Learning: Throughout my journey, I came to understand the invaluable role of mentorship and lifelong learning. Bill, a seasoned businessman, emerged as my mentor, offering guidance and tough love when needed. Embracing the wisdom of Bill and other mentors, I remained dedicated to self-improvement, recognizing the transformative power of continuous learning in shaping both my personal and professional growth.

Accountability and Ownership: As my story unfolded, I learned firsthand the importance of accountability and ownership. Bill's no-

nonsense approach pushed me to confront my decisions and take responsibility for my actions. This principle became ingrained in my ethos, guiding me to hold myself to high standards, learn from my mistakes, and embrace accountability in all aspects of my life, whether personal or business-related.

Actionable Tips

Since I was 23, I've learned a thing or two about navigating life's twists and turns. I've embraced resilience and adaptability as my guiding principles. Along the way, I've had the privilege of learning from mentors like Bill, who taught me the value of continuous learning, accountability, and ownership. Taken straight from my experience, here are a few actionable tips that have served me well on my journey—a journey marked by growth, self-discovery, and the pursuit of excellence.

1. **Seek Mentorship:** Actively seek out mentors who can offer guidance and support as you navigate challenges and opportunities in your personal and professional life. Look for individuals with experience and wisdom who can provide valuable insights and perspective.
2. **Embrace Continuous Learning:** Dedicate yourself to lifelong learning and self-improvement. Be open to new ideas, perspectives, and experiences that can help you grow personally and professionally. Whether through formal education, mentorship, or self-directed learning, commit to expanding your knowledge and skills.
3. **Take Ownership:** Hold yourself accountable for your decisions and actions. Recognize that taking ownership of your choices

empowers you to learn from mistakes, grow as an individual, and ultimately achieve your goals. Embrace a mindset of accountability in both your personal and professional endeavors.

4. **Adaptability and Resilience:** Cultivate adaptability and resilience in the face of challenges and uncertainty. Embrace change as an opportunity for growth, and approach obstacles with a positive attitude and a willingness to learn and adapt. Remember that resilience is a skill that can be developed over time through practice and perseverance.

Connect

Let's connect! You can follow Design It Wraps & Tint on Facebook and Instagram:

- Facebook: www.facebook.com/designitwraps
- Instagram: www.instagram.com/designitwraps

You can also find us directly on our website at designitwraps.com.

ABOUT THE AUTHOR

Brent Knott is the dedicated owner-operator behind Design It Wraps & Tint. Since 2013, Brent and his team at Design It Wraps & Tint have been the go-to experts for vehicle/boat wraps, tinting, vehicle protection, and business signage on the First Coast. Based in Fernandina Beach, Florida, Brent shares his home with his two beloved dogs and his supportive girlfriend. With a passion for craftsmanship and a commitment to customer satisfaction, Brent continues to elevate the standards of quality and service in the custom vehicle wraps and graphics industry.

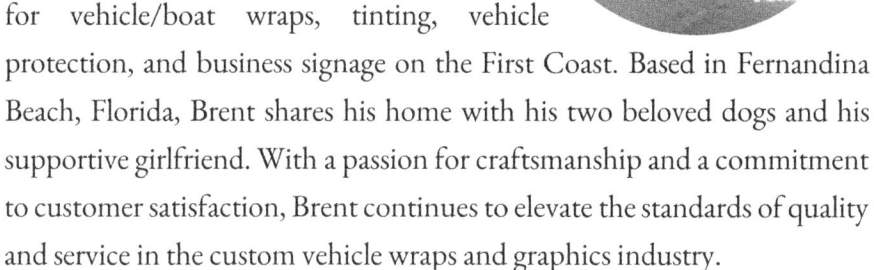

CHAPTER 12

Unleashing Competitive Advantage:

The Power of Growth Marketing for Businesses

by Scott Conway

📝 The Story

It was December 26, 2022, a gloomy Friday night in Medellin, known for its bustling streets and occasional incidents of theft. Stepping out of the Uber, I was greeted by the chaotic energy of the city - taxis vying for passengers, buses rushing by, and people bustling about. Despite the reputation for danger, there was a warmth in the air that made me feel surprisingly safe. As I walked through the mall, burdened by the stress of entrepreneurship that had been weighing on me for the past five years, I couldn't help but smile at the lively atmosphere around me. With my Airpods in, I made my way to the theater, immersed in a mix of Classic Rock and Local Colombian Folk Music. The theater itself was a sight to behold, brightly lit with white stone floors reflecting the light above, and concessions offering treats in Spanish. As I entered Colombia's largest movie theater, located in the hometown of Pablo Escobar, I felt a sense of awe. Tonight, I was here to watch the second Avatar in theaters in 4X Imax, surrounded by gorgeous Colombian couples on their date nights. Although tempted to invite Luisa, I relished the opportunity to enjoy this movie night alone, just for myself.

I arrived at the theater just as the movie was starting. Fast forward, the film captivated me, following Jake Sully's family as they experienced ups and downs, witnessed the war with the humans, and the devastation of Pandora. (SPOILER ALERT) Tears welled in my eyes during the scene where Jake Sully's oldest son passed away in his arms. It made me reflect on my journey and how far I had come. From struggling to make ends meet, earning less than minimum wage in sales for four years, to achieving our second consecutive 7-figure year. How did I find myself in this position?

Jan 2021

Winning clients with our offer became increasingly challenging as the market shifted. They demanded a service we didn't have, despite our attempts to launch it. Unfortunately, we couldn't provide it profitably. Making matters worse, I made the cardinal sin for a service-based business: I lowered our prices. This decision led to a drastic decrease in revenue, from about $50k per month to a mere $20k, and we began to struggle.

To compound our issues, hiring people to help solve these problems for clients became impossible. The clients we attracted were demanding, impatient, and unwilling to put in the necessary work. As a result, I found myself single-handedly managing all aspects of the business: hiring, training, sales, client management, and more. Splitting my energy across these tasks resulted in subpar service delivery, making the situation feel like total hell.

Despite the challenges, my partner and I stubbornly clung to our offer, resisting innovation for six long months. It wasn't until I met Davidson Joseph in Brooklyn that things began to change.

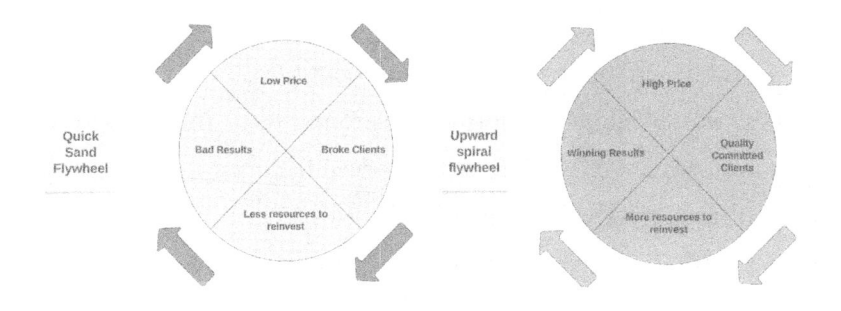

🎯 Principle in Action

Any company is a series of flywheels in action. Our decisions directly impact our future options. For services, pricing/business model is the most impactful input variable which dictates the rest of the business. Services where people are involved in the delivery of service will always have a cost to fulfill. Our ability to create freedom is directly tied to price. More on this later.

Back to the story...

Aug 2021

Meeting Davidson in May 2021 marked a significant turning point for us. As a realtor based in Brooklyn, Davidson introduced us to the concept of sourcing lists of homeowners and how to effectively remarket to them. He had a vision to scale this process, and that's where our marketing expertise came into play. It was precisely the opportunity we had been waiting for.

My business partner Juan and I quickly agreed on the new offer. Just six months prior, what we were selling felt like pulling teeth – there was little demand for our services. I had recognized the need to adapt for some time, but Juan had been more skeptical. With my background in sales and his in tech and marketing, our roles complemented each other well. I handled sales and service fulfillment, while Juan managed clients, marketing, and the technology behind our operations.

The shift was invigorating. Our beta customers were thrilled with the new offer and were even willing to provide references. Our seller lead generation offer perfectly aligned with market demand. We transitioned from selling $250 setups to $5,000 setups, experiencing a surge in demand. Additionally, our niche meme page, boasting 92k followers, became a valuable source of referrals. With the implementation of this high-ticket offer, our growth skyrocketed, generating $46k in monthly revenue within just two months of its launch.

Our next target was to hit $80k in monthly revenue, a milestone I was confident we would achieve in due time. My schedule was packed with sales calls, and I found myself working long hours – often 12 to 14-hour days – overseeing operations and sales. Over the following three months, I took decisive steps to delegate tasks, including recruiting, business administration, customer success, and sales.

This marked a transition into uncharted territory – the beginning of my journey from being comfortable as a salesperson to assuming an executive role.

🎯 Principle in Action

A lot of companies stick to either organic, outbound, or paid acquisition channels. They find what works and then they stop innovating.

Most direct response marketers have media buying backgrounds. Media buyers operate like scientists in a lab. Following linear logic they follow the flowchart below. On the surface this makes sense.

Example of the Conversion Accelerator Formula:

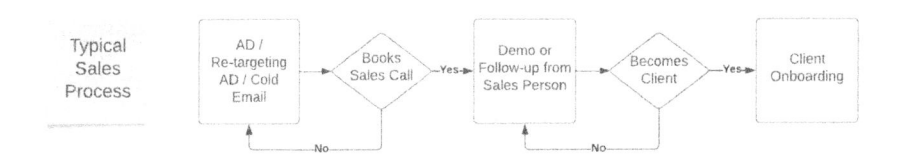

```
Typical        AD /                                  Demo or
Sales      Re-targeting      Books      -Yes->   Follow-up from     Becomes    -Yes->    Client
Process     AD / Cold      Sales Call                Sales Person       Client             Onboarding
              Email
                 ↑                                        ↑
                 └──────────No──────────┘                 └────────No────────┘
```

What do you think might be wrong here?

The traditional approach to sales is fading away. Today, both consumers and businesses expect more from their service providers. They not only seek content that addresses their problems but also demand validation from their peers that the solution is effective. According to a LinkedIn survey, 66% of CEOs base their purchasing decisions on referrals. What does this signify? It underscores the necessity for our marketing efforts to span the entire spectrum, guiding strangers toward becoming enthusiastic prospects eager to engage with our brand.

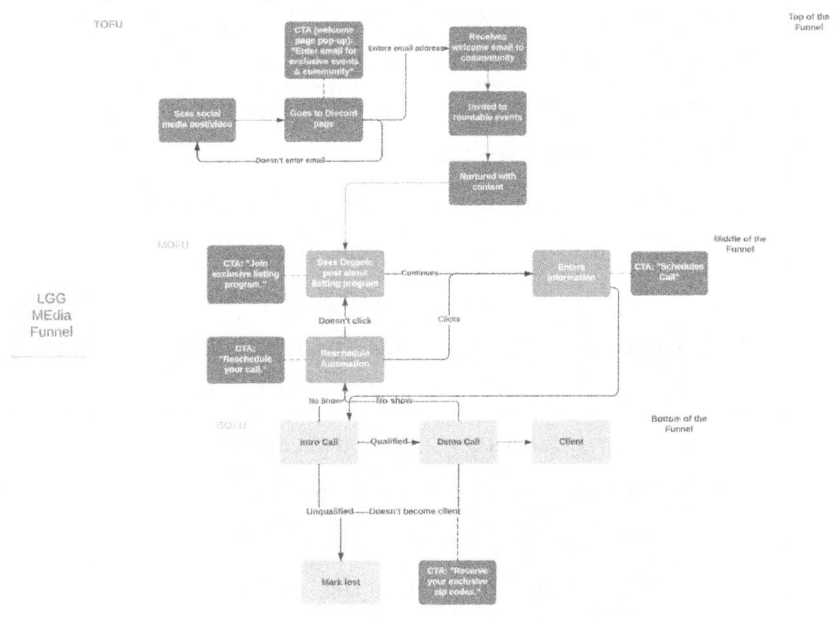

The reason this funnel worked so effectively was our implementation of the Conversion Accelerator Formula.

What makes the conversion funnel accelerator so successful is its ability to address the fundamental question: How can we quickly transform strangers into potential customers who not only like but also trust and respect our brand?

Back to the story...

January 2022

We celebrated our first $138k month, and in doing so, I had effectively delegated myself out of a job.

Becoming an executive was uncharted territory for me. Like Caesar crossing the Rubicon, there was no turning back; the only path was forward. I was determined to figure it out.

"Scott, we're facing pushback from clients regarding the quality of leads," Juan informed me. "If we don't enhance it, we risk losing them."

"Hmm," I pondered. "How can we improve lead quality?" Without reliable metrics, I had no way of gauging our performance beyond client feedback. Realizing our lack of data, I knew we had a major hurdle to overcome. We needed robust internal feedback mechanisms to evaluate how we filtered leads and gather client feedback on each lead sent.

After deliberation, we settled on Google Data Studio, now Looker from Google, to visualize the data. Once Juan completed building the dashboards, the question arose: "What's next? How do we prioritize inputs to influence these customer success indicators?"

Juan emphasized the need for testing. We had to experiment with different scripts and approaches to marketing the service to agents. Despite my initial skepticism about the cost and complexity of implementing effective feedback mechanisms and training our team, I realized the greater cost of not testing.

Indeed, what was the price of missing out on 90% of the available market share by not striving for excellence? Testing and innovation were our pathways to success, even if it meant diving into what some might consider the mundane but profitable aspects of business.

Principle in Action

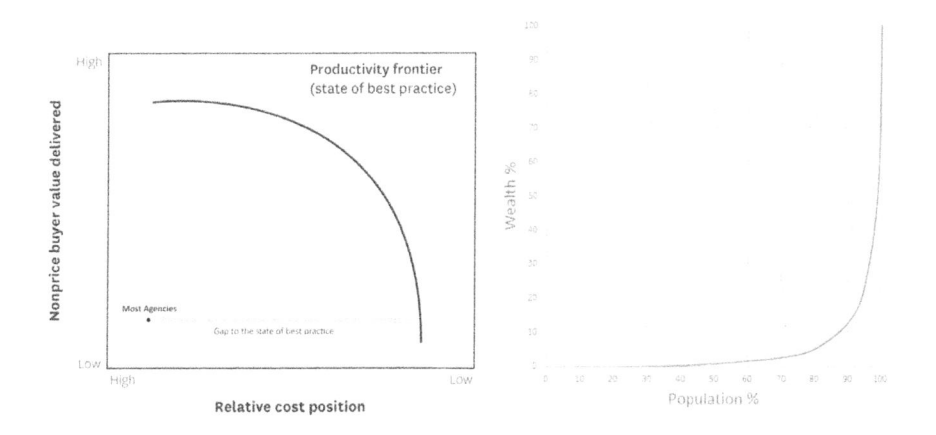

Most businesses in a market tend to trail behind the top performers in adopting best practices. When engaging with our clients, we targeted the top 10% of realtors as our ideal clients. However, even within this segment, there exists a significant disparity between a top 1% realtor and a top 10% realtor. What accounted for this difference?

The top 1% had superior systems that generated a higher output per unit of cost. In other words, they achieved greater results with less effort and expense. They displayed a willingness to invest the necessary effort and refine their systems to attain a level of excellence that the rest of the market was not prepared to pursue.

While this book does not aim to delve into political discourse, it's worth noting that despite the discussions around wealth inequality, a universal observation persists: the top 10% of a market typically secure 90% of its results. The distinguishing factor between the top 10% and the rest lies in their proximity to executing best practices. Therefore, the primary objective of any business should be to swiftly adopt best practices. This can be accomplished through rapid testing and innovation outpacing the rest of the market.

How do we conduct these tests effectively? We maintain all variables in a given process constant while substituting the highest leverage components that we believe may yield the most significant results.

The question then arises: how do we determine which tests to prioritize, and when do we know it's time to conclude them? Stay tuned for the answers.

Back to the story...

June 2022

I found myself overseeing a team of 20 individuals, drowning in a sea of information and tasks. The pace of growth was dizzying, almost overwhelming. Despite this rapid expansion, our recent efforts to expand the team with 14 new hires had faltered. The investment of over $8,000 in training expenses, coupled with the hiring costs and the considerable time spent by the team on interviewing and onboarding, felt like a substantial loss.

Returning home to Ottawa after a grueling 31-hour flight from Dubai, exhaustion weighed heavily on me. Yet, amidst my weariness, I was confronted with a business in turmoil. It was evident that a significant misstep had occurred, prompting me to delve into a thorough root cause analysis.

It became clear that our onboarding process was riddled with inefficiencies and lacked clear priorities for each team member. Determined to rectify this, I undertook the task of refining our approach. By distilling each role within our organization to its core behaviors and aligning them with key performance indicators (KPIs), I restructured our onboarding process.

The impact was immediate and profound. Our revamped onboarding process not only bolstered the quality of leads generated by new hires by a staggering 40% but also slashed our training costs by a remarkable 96%. This strategic overhaul not only addressed our immediate challenges but also laid a solid foundation for sustainable growth and success.

🎯 Principle in Action

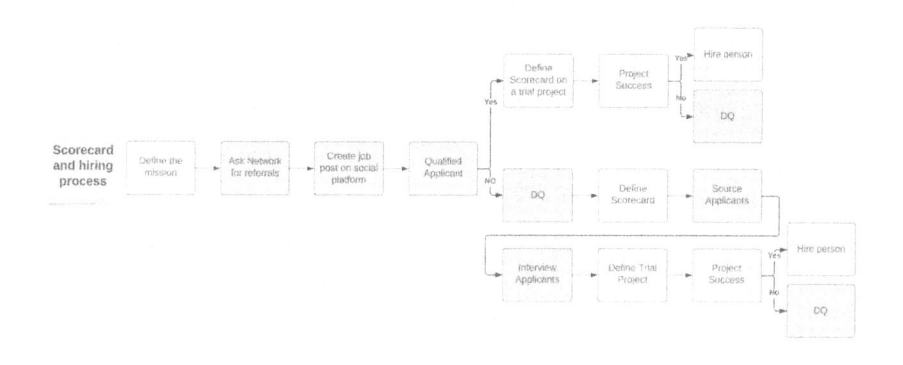

Every role within a company requires a clear and concise scorecard. This scorecard serves as a roadmap, outlining the role's mission – a broad vision that encapsulates what success entails. For instance, consider the mission for an inside salesperson: "To facilitate our clients' acquisition of profitable leads by generating qualified leads who engage and attend appointments related to property sales." Similarly, the mission for a Chief Revenue Officer might be articulated as: "To anticipate future trends and assess necessary adaptations to the Go-To-Market (GTM) strategy and sales process, ensuring ACME Corp remains at the forefront of innovation."

This framework provides a foundational understanding of each role's objectives and responsibilities. The subsequent section of the scorecard focuses on the specific problems that the role is tasked with solving. The approach here is to identify the behaviors directly linked to success in the role and to document them on the scorecard. This process is essential for fostering clarity among management, recruiting partners, and, most importantly, the individuals occupying the role. By distilling the essential behaviors, the scorecard offers clear guidance on where to direct focus and effort, emphasizing quality over quantity in problem-solving approaches.

For example, in the inside sales role we needed them to:

1. Probe with open-ended questions, actively listen to the prospect, and then employ *mirroring* and *labeling* techniques to reflect the sentiments and emotions uncovered during the probing process. This approach served as a cornerstone in teaching emotional intelligence to our globally dispersed sales team, transcending language and cultural barriers. Whether it was a salesperson in their 30s from the Philippines or a 67-year-old homeowner in Brooklyn, our team learned to relate to prospects effectively, fostering deeper connections and understanding.
    a. In his book *Never Split the Difference*, Chris Voss delves into the psychology of achieving 'Yes' in negotiations. He elucidates two pivotal techniques:
        i. *Mirroring* involves echoing the last three words or the most significant detail shared by the prospect. This practice demonstrates active listening and genuine interest in the prospect's perspective.

      ii. *Labeling* entails discerning the prospect's emotions and articulating them back, prefaced by "it sounds like you are feeling [emotion]." This phrasing allows room for correction if the label is inaccurate and fosters empathy towards the prospect.
          1. Bonus: If it's not accurate, and the prospect corrects us, this is a mirroring opportunity. "Oh ok, so you're actually feeling [accurate emotion." Either way, we remain in the driver's seat.
2. Handle objections and understand when the prospect is saying "yes" to get off of the phone.
3. Understand how to tie the prospect's needs into why the prospect should move ahead with the next step of the sales process.
4. Use tonality and communicate like a leader to prospects.
5. Speak with confidence. This should be self-explanatory.

How did we translate this into a scorecard? For more senior positions, we can entrust the task to the individual intended to fill the role. Let them craft their own roadmap to success. The fewer tasks on our plate, the more we can focus on driving impactful change as leaders and executives. This approach thrives when the candidate is referred to us. Should the referral not pan out, we can share this scorecard with our recruitment partners to source potential candidates. However, there are instances when we must shoulder the responsibility ourselves to ensure the role's clarity is crystal clear.

Determine: What are the decisions that the team member needs to make on a day-to-day basis?

Track outcomes:

It either happened or it did not. What are 1-3 metrics or trackable behaviors that are tied to the critical outcomes for the role? For this role it was:

1. **Volume of meetings set**: This showed us how adept they were at probing, mirroring, and closing.
2. **Volume of qualified meetings set**: This showed us how well they did with handling objections.
3. **Talk time** (as measured by the average length of each salesperson's call): This showed us how they performed with leading, probing, and mirroring.

Back to the story...

Oct 2022

Everything in our business fulfillment had stabilized, but I still felt overwhelmed by the sheer volume of tasks. I found myself devoting an exorbitant amount of time to business administration and keeping the team organized. What made matters worse was the growing divide between my business partner and me. For the past three years, we had been operating separate lines of business. He had expressed his desire to hand off the real estate division to me entirely, but at the time, I didn't fully grasp the implications. Looking back, I realized that as leaders, we were inadvertently creating two bottlenecks in the business.

Our inability to scale ourselves resulted in mounting tension and friction in our relationship. I sought marketing and data support to decipher the business trends, yet encountered resistance from my partner with vague responses like "it can't be done" or "it's not feasible," without elaboration. Frustrated by these half-hearted answers, I questioned why we maintained a 50/50 partnership. I was putting in maximum effort, striving to address the business's needs, only to be met with constant roadblocks. Despite my attempts to guide him through the hiring process and implement effective management strategies, he remained reluctant to relinquish control or explore more efficient methods of operation.

During this challenging period, I endeavored to be a supportive partner. I sought guidance from an emotional intelligence coach to manage my anger and invested $10k in enhancing my knowledge of marketing and management, hoping to make a more significant contribution to our company. While I wasn't flawless and struggled with prioritization, I may have unwittingly contributed to the proliferation of non-essential tasks that consumed valuable time. Over half of my week was spent navigating our project management software, signaling an underlying issue.

As I continued to dedicate considerable time to administrative tasks, I noticed diminishing returns across various aspects of our business. The real estate market had undergone a significant shift, with a slowdown attributed to rising interest rates. Our revenue, closely tied to existing home sales in the US and Canada, mirrored this decline, plummeting approximately 30% since January 2022 in the US and up to 66% in certain Canadian markets.

United States Existing Home Sales

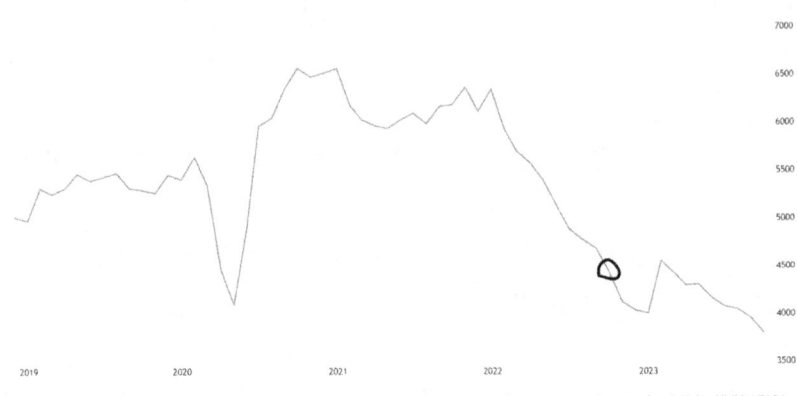

Summary Stats Forecast Calendar Alerts Download ▼

[Chart showing US Existing Home Sales from 2019 to 2023, ranging between 3500 and 7000, with a circled point near 2023 around 4500]

TRADINGECONOMICS.COM | NATIONAL ASSOCIATION OF REALTORS

I was overwhelmed by doubts and teetering on the edge of burnout. There were countless moments throughout the year when it would have been tempting to abandon our line of business. The challenges mentioned above offer just a glimpse into our tumultuous journey, but despite it all, we persevered. I refused to let go of my commitment to my partner and our team. Even as market dynamics shifted from a seller's market to a more balanced one, our team relied on us.

My partner and I knew we had to find a solution together, one that would benefit everyone involved—the clients, the team, and the business alike.

🎯 Principle in Action

While I was certainly busy, much of my effort lacked meaningful impact on the business. This experience taught me a valuable lesson: at any given time, a business faces only five constraints (shown below). Prioritizing the right constraint at the wrong time is still a misstep. Therefore, if there's one key

148

takeaway from this book, let it be this: focus on addressing one constraint at a time and make it your primary objective. Our ability to scale to seven figures within five months was a direct result of getting this principle right. However, when we deviated from this approach, our progress stalled and profits declined.

1. Lead Generation
2. Lead Nurture
3. Sales
4. Fulfillment/ops bandwidth
5. Account Growth/Ascension

In action, this looks like blocking off the first part of the day and focusing on the one selected constraint within the business and solving it. Repeat this daily, until the constraint has been solved.

Motion

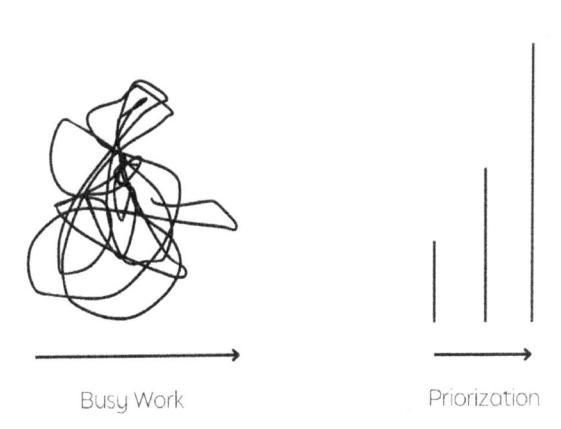

Busy Work | Priorization

Prioritization demands less energy than multitasking and juggling numerous tasks, yet it produces superior results.

Back to the story...

Jan 2023

First, my partner and I spent three weeks renegotiating our operating agreement. I was set to rejoin our marketing attribution and media buying arm. With realignment achieved, we were back on track, and I had a new mission.

Terms were agreed upon, and the exit was finalized. We had arranged for one of our clients to acquire our sales team, while a separate buyer was secured for our client list. Ensuring the buyer for the client list had a proven track record and could meet our clients' needs satisfactorily was paramount. After three years of dedication and hard work, terms for the exit were settled.

Completing the first exit, especially under 30, brought me immense satisfaction.

🔗 Connect

Ready to take your business to the next level? Gain access to my exclusive free training on a proven 6-month roadmap to achieving $100k/mo profit! Don't miss out on this opportunity for valuable insights and strategies. Visit breadinc.io/organic to get started today.

ABOUT THE AUTHOR

Scott Conway is an accomplished international executive with business experience spanning Canada, USA, Colombia, South Africa, the Philippines, and Nigeria. Achieving a successful exit under 30, he brings a wealth of expertise to the table. His core competencies include sales, sales operations, creative marketing, analytics, and optimizing business operations for efficiency and cost-effectiveness. With a proven track record of leading both small and large teams, Scott is fluent in English and Spanish.

In his leisure time, Scott delves into the exploration of consciousness through meditation and mindfulness practices, enjoys attending comedy shows, and embarks on adventures around the globe. He also is also an art enthusiast, and by art enthusiast he really means tattoo connoisseur.

CONCLUSION

As we come to the close of this journey through the trials and triumphs of the business world, I am reminded of the remarkable resilience, ingenuity, and determination that characterize the entrepreneurial spirit. From the poignant narratives shared by our respected contributors to the actionable tips and strategies they've imparted, *Real Talk With Real Business Pros: How To Win In A Competitive Marketplace* serves as a testament to the boundless potential that lies within each of us to succeed in a competitive marketplace.

Throughout the chapters of this book, we've explored the myriad challenges and opportunities that define the business landscape—from navigating market disruptions to fostering innovation, from overcoming setbacks to seizing moments of triumph. At every turn, our authors have offered candid insights gleaned from their own experiences, illuminating key principles of success that transcend industry boundaries and organizational hierarchies.

As you reflect on the stories and lessons shared within these pages, I encourage you to consider the broader implications for your own entrepreneurial journey. What obstacles do you face in your pursuit of success? What opportunities lie waiting to be seized? How can you apply the principles and strategies outlined in this book to your own endeavors, whether big or small?

Remember that success in the competitive arena of business is not a destination but a journey—a journey marked by perseverance, adaptability, and a relentless pursuit of excellence. Embrace the challenges that lie ahead as opportunities for growth, and approach each day with the same tenacity and determination that have guided the authors of this book on their own paths to success.

As you chart your course forward, know that you are not alone. Draw inspiration from the stories of those who have walked this path before you, and lean on the wisdom and support of your fellow entrepreneurs and business professionals. Together, we can overcome any obstacle, surmount any challenge, and achieve greatness beyond measure.

So here's to you, dear reader—to your resilience, your ambition, and your unwavering commitment to excellence. May the lessons learned from the pages of this book guide you on your journey to success, and may you continue to thrive and prosper in the competitive landscape of business.

Renee Lautermilch
Chief Editor
Smart Publishing

ABOUT SMART PUBLISHING

Back in 2021, Jonathan Lautermilch was introduced to the idea of becoming an author through a mastermind he had joined.

His mentor in the mastermind had built multiple 8-figure businesses through the books he had authored over the years.

In fact, one of these books was how Jonathan ended up becoming his client and mentee in the first place.

Initially, he was hesitant…

He pondered,

"Is this the right move for me and my business?"

"Will it work for me the way it has for my mentor?"

"If I pursue this, I know nothing about writing or publishing a book. How will I even get started, much less finish?"

And most of all, he wondered…

"Is my story even worth sharing?"

What ultimately spurred him into action?

It was the compelling evidence from his peers in the mastermind who were becoming published authors. It was just too convincing to ignore.

So he engaged a publisher and embarked on the journey of writing his first book: *Groomed For Greatness: How to Get What You're Worth as a Fitness Professional*.

Although the book was successful, Jonathan fell short of reaching bestseller status. Why? The publisher he hired lacked expertise in the realm of book marketing and business strategy.

Despite this, the book proved immensely successful, adding multiple six figures to his business's bottom line.

Inspired by Jonathan's achievement, his wife, Renee, decided to self-publish her first book. This decision allowed them to gain intimate knowledge of the publishing business, from the intricacies of manuscript development and publishing to the pivotal details that distinguish an ordinary book from one that achieves Amazon Bestseller status upon release.

After "cracking the code," they began receiving inquiries from other business owners and CEOs seeking their assistance in publishing their books and achieving bestseller status. And thus, Smart Publishing was born.

Smart Publishing boasts a 100% success rate in creating bestselling authors.

Their mission is to empower 1000 business owners to become bestselling authors, enabling them to dominate their marketplace and leave a lasting legacy.

Ready to turn your book dream into reality? Whether you're an aspiring author or a seasoned entrepreneur with a story to share, let Smart Publishing guide you on the path to success. Our proven expertise and 100% success rate in creating bestselling authors ensure that your book receives the recognition it deserves. Don't let uncertainty hold you back—take the first step toward becoming a bestselling author and dominating your marketplace.

Contact us today to learn how we can help you unleash your book's potential and leave a lasting legacy.

SMART PUBLISHING

go.thesmartshark.com/book-publishing-homepage

Made in the USA
Monee, IL
02 April 2024